AMERICAN GEORGIAN
ARCHITECTURE

Books by the same authors:

PRACTICAL BOOK OF GARDEN STRUCTURE AND DESIGN, 1937

COLONIAL INTERIORS, 3RD SERIES, 1938

PORTRAIT OF A COLONIAL CITY ; PHILADELPHIA 1670-1838, 1939

HISTORIC HOUSES OF THE HUDSON VALLEY, 1942

DIARY OF INDEPENDENCE HALL, 1948

By Harold Donaldson Eberlein:

LITTLE KNOWN ENGLAND, 1930

THE ENGLISH INN, PAST AND PRESENT (*with*
A. E. Richardson, R.A.), 1925

THE SMALLER ENGLISH HOUSE OF THE LATER RENAISSANCE
(*with A. E. Richardson, R.A.*), 1925

*This is one of a Series of Illustrated Monographs on various aspects of Georgian Architecture and Decoration,
at home and abroad. The Series is under the general editorship of the
Publications Sub-Committee of the Georgian Group.*

FAIRMOUNT WATER WORKS, Philadelphia. 1822

AMERICAN GEORGIAN ARCHITECTURE

by

HAROLD DONALDSON EBERLEIN

and

CORTLANDT VAN DYKE HUBBARD

Line Drawings

by

JOHN B. LEAR, Jr.

LONDON: PLEIADES BOOKS LIMITED

1952

To

MARGARET DOUGLAS HUBBARD

First published in 1952 by
Pleiades Books Ltd., 11 Fitzroy Square, London, W. 1
and printed in Great Britain by
Robert MacLehose & Co. Ltd., The University Press, Glasgow

CONTENTS

ILLUSTRATIONS IN THE TEXT

ILLUSTRATIONS IN THE TEXT

LIST OF PLATES

xi

All photographs, unless otherwise credited, were made by
C. V. D. HUBBARD

THE MEDIAEVAL BEGINNINGS

To UNDERSTAND AMERICAN Georgian architecture, one must know something of what preceded it. Long before any trace of Renaissance influence appeared in the American Colonies, architecture was of different Mediaeval derivations. Utterly distinct types—English, Dutch, Flemish, Swedish and, later, German—resulted from the artisans naturally trying at first to follow the wonted building practices of their several homelands. Each of these regional types was highly individual.

We must reckon the diverse racial origins in the several colonies. In the South (the Carolinas, Virginia and Maryland) the people were English. In Virginia and Maryland they remained wholly English for more than a hundred years; not until well into the eighteenth century did numerous Scots-Irish and Germans enter the western parts of both colonies. In South Carolina, the few Dutch and Huguenots who came at the beginning of colonisation were soon absorbed but left perceptible traces on the earliest types of construction, especially in some of the middling urban building (in Charleston) and in a few instances in the country. The English Barbadians brought with them certain features they had picked up in their previous West Indian experience, such as verandahs and porticoes.

In the Middle Colonies, the Dutch and Swedes came first into what afterwards became Pennsylvania and South Jersey. The Swedes introduced to the western world the log cabin built of logs laid horizontally, a structure without precedent in English tradition. From 1664 onward, under the Duke of York's Government, English colonists came gradually into the territory and also took up lands in East and West Jersey under the Berkeley and Carteret proprietary grants. The planting of Newark by New England Puritans in 1666, and of Burlington by the Quakers in 1672, hastened English colonisation in the Jerseys.

When Charles II granted William Penn the Proprietary Province of Pennsylvania in 1681, the swelling tide of English and Welsh immigration soon absorbed the readily assimilable Swedes. Thenceforth the Welsh stone farmhouse or *hendre* rapidly multiplied throughout the Welsh Barony of Pennsylvania. In New Castle, Kent and Sussex, the 'Three Lower Counties upon Delaware' (the present State of Delaware), the people were entirely English save for the few Swedes and fewer Dutch previously settled there. And the English had been recruited, too, from Maryland before the Duke of York transferred his rights to Penn.

Although some German colonists had reached Penn's 'Holy Experiment' before the end of the seventeenth century, not until about the second decade of the eighteenth did great waves of Germans begin to cause the Provincial authorities concern; Council and Assembly feared it would be well-nigh impossible to assimilate them. On the heels of the Germans came hordes of Scots-Irish who settled on the Provincial frontiers.

New York and North Jersey (Nieuw Nederland at first) were Dutch and Flemish from the outset, with a sprinkling of Walloons and Huguenots. The Dutch were numerically and politically preponderant, but there were more Flemings than is generally realised. They were especially numerous in southern New York and north-eastern Jersey. Even after 1664, when Nieuw Nederland came under British rule and the territory was granted the Duke of York as the Province of New York, the Dutch, Flemings and Walloons long remained the majority of the population, notwithstanding the many English who straightway migrated to New York City or settled on the great manorial grants along the Hudson and in Westchester County. The western half of the Long Island part of the Province became partly Dutch, partly English; the eastern half, settled mainly by Connecticut people, was altogether English and, even to-day, it is more like Connecticut in character than like the rest of New York. The Walloons and Huguenots, in Westchester County and elsewhere in the Province, soon merged with the rest of the population.

New England—the territory now comprising Connecticut, Rhode Island, Massachusetts, New Hampshire, Vermont and Maine—was entirely English from the outset and has remained English, save for a very recent inundation of Canadian French and some Poles and Portuguese in a few districts.

In course of time the early regional and racial types of architecture underwent inevitable modifications (figs. D and E). These came gradually as experience of local conditions dictated now this change, now that, from the first attempts to reproduce

2

exactly the familiar methods and types of the parent lands. Local conditions embraced climate, the materials most readily available and the economic factors that influenced or determined the social structures of the several colonies. Traditional preferences, too, played their part when increasing prosperity and other circumstances permitted a choice of materials and methods.

THE SOUTH

IN VIRGINIA AND Maryland the earliest dwellings were Mediaeval in structure and aspect—notably so at Jamestown and St. Mary's. Although the first Jamestown efforts to provide shelter in 1607 produced only flimsy makeshifts, by 1611 we have record of habitations whose architectural parentage is clearly identifiable. Save for the brick tower of the old church, Jamestown long ago perished utterly because of successive disastrous fires and subsequent abandonment on removing the seat of Government to Williamsburg. At St. Mary's, only two of the early permanent dwellings survive, *St. Peter's Key* and *Clocker's Fancy*—both of them much altered and the former sadly dilapidated.

Nevertheless, it has been possible to determine accurately the outward appearance, plan and methods of construction of these vanished and long-forgotten buildings. Careful digging on the sites has revealed much that for generations was believed irretrievably lost. Not only have the unearthed foundations disclosed valuable evidence, but meticulous sifting of the earth has yielded rich store of roofing and paving tiles, and some faience wall tiles; bricks, both common and gauged or moulded; latches, hinges, pintles, casement stays, frames, saddle-bars, nails and other bits of hardware; broken glass, both quarries and lozenges, and portions of lead calmes; and even fragments of plaster sufficient to reconstruct the pattern of some of the polychromed pargework from several of the more important houses. Documentary evidence complements and confirms the deductions drawn from excavation. The evidence is convincing beyond all peradventure that the early dwellings at Jamestown, St. Mary's, and elsewhere in Virginia and Maryland were of half-timber construction like contemporary houses in England, the panels between posts and studs filled with 'wattle and daub' work or brick nogging, the outside either left with the timbers exposed or else covered with plaster or, as an alternative to plaster, a sheathing of weather-boarding or clapboards nailed to the posts and studs. In his *Jamestown and St. Mary's* (Johns Hopkins Press, 1938), Henry Chandlee Forman gives the whole fascinating story in detail.

Complete brick walls, too—laid in either English or Flemish bond (Pl. 2)—appeared at an early date. One still surviving brick instance of Mediaeval building tradition perpetuated in Virginia appears in St. Luke's Church (Pl. 1), Smithfield, Isle of Wight County, built about 1632. Although documentary evidence is lacking to support this date, in this case tradition seems particularly credible.

THE MIDDLE COLONIES

IN THE DELAWARE Valley region, now embracing Delaware, south-eastern Pennsylvania and South Jersey, the earliest dwellings that may date from the days of Dutch and Swedish rule (1623-64) are the tiny *Old Dutch House* in New Castle (Delaware) that might, perhaps, antedate the Duke of York's Government, and the older part of the *Cannon Ball House*, in the Passyunk district of Philadelphia, built almost certainly between 1658 and 1660.

The really active period of building in and around Philadelphia, and in Bucks, Chester and the 'Three Lower Counties', did not begin until Charles II granted Penn the Proprietary Province in 1681. By that time new ideals in building had almost wholly supplanted Mediaeval tradition. Even the stone farmhouses, the *hendres*, in Pennsylvania's Welsh Barony, such as *Pencoyd* or the older parts of *Maen Coch*, *Pont Redding* or *Wynnestay*, reflected the new influences. All this phase of Middle Colonies architecture, therefore, belongs to a later chapter.

The only instances of Mediaeval structure in Pennsylvania belong chronologically in the mid-eighteenth century. Built by the German immigrants, who persistently remained a 'people apart' and clung tenaciously to their language and traditional culture, they are all in what were called in the eighteenth century the 'back parts' of the Province and occur within a relatively small area. The most significant examples are the Sisters' House and 'Saal' of the Seventh-Day Baptists' community at Ephrata. Of half-timber construction, with stone and clay-plaster filling between studs and diagonal braces, several tiers of 'watershed' dormers, and tiny casement windows, their whole aspect recalls 'the Germany of Albrecht Dürer'. Of similar construction also is the old Moravian Mission House in the Oley Valley near Reading.

North Jersey, Newark and Elizabeth, settled as they were by New England colonists, in the seventeenth century continued the Mediaeval usages then current in New England.

In early seventeenth-century New York City (Nieuw Amsterdam) the brick or stone houses, their crow-stepped parapets and gable-ends to the street, were exact counterparts of contemporary dwellings in Holland, where domestic architecture was still Mediaeval. So far as they could, the Dutch transplanted with punctilious exactitude every feature of their culture. What was true of building in the little town of Nieuw Amsterdam was true in Fort Orange (Albany) and true, also, in the settlements between the two. Although crow-stepped and curvilinear gables seem not to have occurred in the country settlements, the houses there exhibited the other Dutch characteristics—the steep-pitched roofs, the tumbled brickwork or 'mouse-tooth' *motif* and kneelers of the straight-lined gables, the finials, the curiously-wrought beam-anchors, the monial windows with leaded casements and shutters below the transoms. The chief difference from town houses was in having the door in the long side instead of the gable-end.

Perhaps as good an example of the early Dutch brick house as any now remaining is *Fort Crailo* (Pl. 6) at Rensselaer, one of the Van Rensselaer houses built about 1642. It had fallen into an almost ruinous condition when the State of New York restored it (not so intelligently as it might) a few years ago. Nevertheless, the distinguishing features are preserved, though one could wish greater accuracy in details.

FIG. A. Flemish 'flying gutter'. North Jersey and Southern New York

A good example of the early Hudson River Dutch stone dwelling is the older part of Pieter Bronck's house (1663) at West Coxsackie (Pl. 7). Other early Dutch stone houses at Old Hurley, and in the Dutch and Huguenot village of New Paltz (Pl. 7), typify the prevalent local methods of building. New Paltz has changed but little since Governour Sir Edmund Andros confirmed the grants and purchase from the Indians. Being exceedingly conservative, the Dutch and Huguenots clung to their seventeenth-century methods, with little or no change, until well into the eighteenth century.

The Flemings, especially numerous in the south-eastern part of the Province—the west shore of the Hudson and the adjacent parts of what is now North Jersey (Bergen and Essex Counties)—indicated their whereabouts by a Flemish type of house whose most conspicuous feature was the so-called 'flying gutter' (fig. A), a bell-wise flare of the roof at the eaves, curving outward sometimes for two feet or more over the front and rear walls 'like the visor of a cap'. West of the Hudson, these Flemish houses were usually built of the local brown sandstone. On Long Island, where stone was scarce, the Flemings fell back on their wonted clay and straw filler for timber framework, oftentimes with a sheathing of long shingles.

NEW ENGLAND

OF SUCH TEMPORARY shelters as the first New England colonists contrived, we know little nor—aside from the record of hardships endured—does it much matter what like were the various rude arrangements their ingenuity prompted them to improvise.

Their first permanent habitations—structures intended to endure, no matter how small—were of distinctly Mediaeval provenance. In their scholarly and exhaustive antiquarian studies of early Connecticut and Rhode Island architecture, Norman M. Isham and Albert F. Brown note that the first artisans were all 'descendants of the Mediaeval craftsmen', and 'had learned their trades . . . under men imbued with what was left of the Mediaeval spirit'. The old joiners and masons were 'of the class whose ideas change slowly'. Trained under masters 'as slow to change as themselves', they had left England before Renaissance ideas had wholly supplanted the old Gothic traditions. Consequently, the houses they built 'were constructed with posts and studs', the panels between which they filled with 'wattle and daub' plastering or with brick nogging. In short, they used the 'old English half-timbered construction with which they were familiar'. The houses they built had their exact counterparts in the

6

English countryside—overhanging upper storeys with carved or moulded pendant 'drops', latticed windows and chamfered or moulded beams with carved stops.

Whether a sheathing of horizontal clapboards or weatherboarding (after the manner the colonists had known in East Anglia, Essex and Sussex) was used from the beginning, it is impossible to say; there is good reason to believe that the outer walls of at least some of the earliest houses lacked sheathing and showed the panels between posts, studs and diagonal braces filled with brick nogging or plaster.

The overhang (Pl. 8) appeared in varied ways—sometimes for one wall only, sometimes for more. The framed overhang usually had greater projection than the moulded overhang. Use of the overhang was more general than is commonly imagined; in sundry instances—especially when a shallow moulded overhang had but slight projection—it has been covered when new clapboarding has been applied. New clapboards have also hidden evidence of alterations when ranges of leaded casements were replaced in the eighteenth century by taller and narrower sashed windows.

In the Providence Plantation of Rhode Island, another mode of construction—its origin has never been fully determined—was used for many of the early houses instead of the half-timber method. Studs were eliminated and the exterior walls were vertically boarded, the heavy upright boards or planks fastened to cills and girts. It was really an adaptation of the old English way of building with 'punches' or puncheons. This mode of construction occasionally appeared elsewhere in the Colonies.

Most of the early New England houses were small. Some, indeed, had only one room downstairs (fig. B, 1), with perhaps another small room in a lean-to at one side;

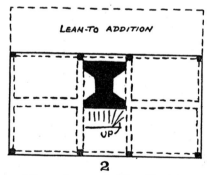
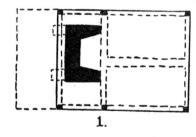

FIG. B. (1) Ground-floor plan, early New England end-chimney one-room to a floor house. Dotted line beyond chimney indicates possible lean-to addition.

FIG. B. (2) Ground-floor plan, early New England central-chimney two-room to a floor house, with possible lean-to addition a massive end-chimney of stone (or, later, of brick) with a spacious fireplace and a winding stair at one side of the chimney-breast; and a single bedchamber above. More usually, there was a central chimney (fig. B, 2); a shallow entry with a three-flight winding stair backed up against the chimney masonry; two rooms downstairs, with fireplaces, and perhaps a third room in a lean-to at the rear; and the plan above-stairs the same, a third chamber in the rear lean-to (if there was one) having its floor lowered several steps because of the roof slope which, otherwise, would have left too little head-room.

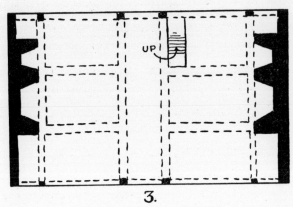

3.

FIG. B. (3) Ground-floor plan, early New England two-chimney two-room to a floor house, with separate central passage

However, as early as 1640 there were a few large houses such as Governour Theophilus Eaton's, the Reverend John Davenport's, Thomas Gregson's or Isaac Allerton's in New Haven. The exceptional wealth in the New Haven Plantation made these houses possible. Governour Eaton's house (demolished before 1730) was built on the ancient English E plan. The Davenport house was 'built in the form of a cross; with the chimney in the centre'. The Gregson and Allerton houses were equally out-standing; the latter is said to have had 'four porches' so was presumably built on the cross-plan. Unfortunately, these large timber-built New Haven houses of the first half of the seventeenth century have all vanished.

Although timber construction was the usual method of building in early New England, there were occasional exceptions when the walls were of brick or stone—for instance, the Spencer-Pierce-Little house at Newbury, with its Mediaeval porch and porch chamber, or the L-shaped stone Whitfield house near the green at Guilford, in Connecticut. Since it was built, in 1640, the latter has undergone so many successive alterations that it is now impossible to determine what was its original interior arrangement. The same thing has befallen the Bull house at Newport, a stone house of about the same date, and other similar instances could be cited.

In all the Colonies, each different racial element left a distinct impress on the local architecture, and in the several Colonies truly *Colonial* types (figs. D and E) evolved through the gradual modification of traditional forms. When greater sophistication came with the advent of the Georgian Age, numerous naïve attempts to graft Georgian features on the different earlier stocks gave rise to a diversity of hybrid forms, difficult to classify exactly but oftentimes virile and satisfying, as well as highly individual.

LATER RENAISSANCE—EARLY GEORGIAN BUILDING

SOON AFTER THE middle of the seventeenth century, while virtually Mediaeval building methods still obtained, a new impulse was felt in several of the Colonies. Increasing prosperity moved the more affluent to building ventures, both individual and corporate, suitable to their means; knowing the architectural trend at home in England, they wished to emulate that vogue so far as they could in a new land. But evidences of the new drift were only sporadic. Natural conservatism, lack of artisans familiar with changed requirements and—except in rare instances—absence of sufficient wealth, all alike favoured perpetuation of the old order. Not least of all, so far as the *small* house was concerned, there was no Renaissance precedent; the contemporary small house in England was spiritually closer akin to Chaucer than to Wren. Even after the new order had won acclaim towards the end of the century, there were frequent overlappings and occasionally, indeed, deliberate reversions to former types as late as the first quarter of the eighteenth century.

THE SOUTH

ADAM THOROUGHGOOD'S HOUSE (Princess Anne County, Virginia), built between 1636 and 1640 (Pl. 2), is one of the comfortable but small houses erected when moderately easy circumstances enabled the owner to have a substantial brick domicile, adequate for a prosperous planter's amenities of living. Plantation houses like Thoroughgood's—there be many in Virginia and Maryland, built in the seventeenth and early eighteenth centuries—may seem to us too small for decent living, but kitchen, servants' quarters and the like were in separate small buildings, the master's dwelling the chief unit of the group. These houses are deceptive in appearance; within they are far roomier than they seem from outside. Wills and inventories of the period prove that many were comfortably if not, indeed, elegantly furnished; the Southern gentry abiding in them were used to as much comfort and elegancy of living as contemporary gentlefolk in England. Museum directors and wealthy collectors to-day are jubilant whenever they can despoil any of these houses of their fine woodwork.

The dormers of Thoroughgood's house are presumably later additions; double-hung sashed windows have replaced the original leaded casements. Otherwise, this house with steep-pitched roof and massive projecting chimney (11 feet wide at base) is little changed since Adam Thoroughgood willed it to his wife in 1640, the counterpart of many a farmhouse of the time in England. The original plan (fig. C)—a central

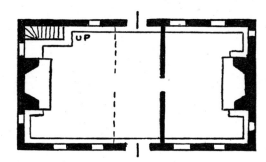

FIG. C. Typical Early Southern Plan; first one partition, then second added making a central hall

doorway opening into the hall or general living-place, a smaller room partitioned off at one end—recalls Mediaeval precedent. The same plan is common in seventeenth-century 1½-storey Virginia and Maryland houses. The next development was to have a second partition, making two equal-sized rooms, one on each side of a wide hall. Climate soon dictated a door at each end of the hall; left open in hot weather, there would be a welcome draught of air. This plan of central hall with doors at each end continued after they began to build houses two rooms deep. Had the original leaded casements remained in these houses, their Mediaeval quality would now have been strikingly evident; later substitution of sashes, oftentimes with enlargement of openings, totally altered their pristine aspect.

Many seventeenth and early eighteenth-century 1½-storey Maryland houses had brick gable-ends, or one brick gable-end, the other walls weatherboarded. Oftentimes a noteworthy feature was the chimney-pent (fig. D); it flourished especially in St. Mary's County, where it apparently originated, but occurs also elsewhere in Maryland and occasionally in Virginia. Attached to a great projecting chimney or, more usually, built between a pair of such chimneys, the brick penthouse had a sloping brick roof. Outwardly, it served as chimney buttress; within doors it provided a deep recess (generally utilised as a cupboard) and sometimes there was a window in the penthouse wall.

Fig. D. Typical St. Mary's County chimney-pent. This type of 1½ storey brick-end house developed early in Southern Maryland. Rarely found elsewhere

Greenspring, which Governour Sir William Berkeley built about 1642 and occupied until his recall in 1677, was the one large brick house built in Virginia before the political unrest of the period halted architectural advance both at home and in the Colonies. Nearly 100 feet long, with an ell at one end, it was a conservative Jacobean structure tinctured with a modicum of Renaissance features. It was demolished when Latrobe was commissioned to build a new house on the site.

In contrast with smaller dwellings, and one of the first evidences of the new trend, is 'Bacon's Castle' (Surry County, Virginia), built by Arthur Allen some time between 1650 and 1660 (Pls, 2, 3), almost the only 'Transitional' surviving house of such early date. More elaborate, possibly, than most of its contemporaries, it is typical in size and probably exemplifies houses built by the wealthier Virginia planters of the second half of the seventeenth century; compared with Thoroughgood's house, it marks a distinct advance in domestic architecture. Within are fine timbered ceilings with richly moulded beams. Barring replacement of the original mullioned and tran-

12

somed windows with their leaded casements by double-hung sashes, and a nineteenth-century extension to the northeast, 'Bacon's Castle' is a 'miraculous survival of a Jacobean Colonial dwelling'. Other early instances of the cross plan occur in both Virginia and Maryland (fig. E).

Of much the same vintage is the Maryland State House (Pls. 3, 4) at St. Mary's, built in 1676; it shows the still vigorous influence of Jacobean tradition unaffected by Later Renaissance features. The old Treasury in Annapolis (1737) shows the cross plan, steep-pitched roof and leaded casements—an architectural 'hold-over' from the previous century.

FIG. E. Bond Castle, Calvert County, Maryland. Built on land granted Sir John Bond in 1649. Cross plan, free-standing chimneys, overhangs, porch with turned spindles, and porch chamber. Originally had leaded casements. Now demolished

Fairfield (Gloucester County), in 1692, is another link in the evolution to Renaissance practice in Virginia. Though a massive chimney, with diagonally-set triple stacks, savours of 'Transitional' usage, the hipped roof has appeared with all it connotes. The unfortunate burning of *Fairfield* in 1897 leaves much uncertainty about its characteristics. One thing, however, is clear—the influence of Sir Christopher Wren had definitely begun to work. But thirteen years before *Fairfield* was built, *Bachelor's Hope* (Pl. 5), in St. Mary's County, Maryland (1679), had given plain evidence that Later Renaissance inspiration—albeit crudely interpreted in the inset portico and clumsily executed Classic details—had penetrated and made itself felt in Lord Baltimore's Province of *Terra Mariae*. The older part of *Holly Hill* (Pl. 18), in Anne Arundel County, built towards the end of the seventeenth century, is another witness to the permeating new impulse in Maryland.

The 'great building' of William and Mary College (Pl. 9) at Williamsburg, begun in 1695, established full ascendancy for the Later Renaissance manner of Wren and his school. The design, commonly attributed (on trustworthy indications) to Sir Christopher himself, shows every characteristic of late seventeenth-century building in England. The '*Wren Building*', usually so called, probably had the first double-hung sash windows in the Colonies.

Scarce three years after the '*Wren Building*' had been started, a disastrous fire at Jamestown (which sealed the doom of the old capital) caused the Assembly to pass 'An Act directing the building of the Capitoll (Pl. 10) and the City of *Williamsburgh*', and to give meticulous directions about the structure 'for ever hereafter to be called and knowne by the Name of the Capitoll of this his Mat^{ies} Colony and Dominion of Virg^a'. Henry Cary, who had been 'overseer' for the erection of William and Mary College, was appointed to the same post for the *Capitol*. The Assembly held their first meeting in the *Capitol* in 1704, before it was entirely finished.

While the *Capitol* was still a-building, plans were afoot for the *Governour's Palace* (Pl. 11). April 30, 1706, a committee from the House of Burgesses waited upon the Governour and 'desired His Excellency . . . to cause a draught' of the proposed house to be laid before them. An Act of October, 1705, had already provided that the *Governour's Palace* be

> 'built of brick, fifty four foot in length, and forty eight foot in breadth, from inside to inside, two storeys high, with convenient cellars underneath and one vault, sash windows, of sash, glass, and a covering of stone slate. . . .'

From the Burgesses' desire for a draught, and from indications in the record of its building, there is ground to believe 'the Palace was designed in London'. In his able work, *The Mansions of Virginia, 1706-76*, Thomas Tileston Waterman points out that the *Palace* design 'would most logically have come from . . . the Office of Works', that Wren was still Surveyor, and that if the Governour of Virginia had applied to the Office of Works, 'Wren himself was likely to have taken the matter under advisement'.

Whether Sir Christopher designed the *Governour's Palace* (as appears credible) or not, it was the 'first of the Virginia houses to have real academic character' and it 'initiated a period of mansion building unequalled in the history of England's Colonies'. With the example of the *Palace* before them, and under assured and increasingly favourable economic conditions, the great Virginia landowners soon sought to build houses becoming their estate, and they naturally turned to England for guidance.

Into English domestic architecture Wren's genius had infused convincing breadth and simplicity without in any wise sacrificing individuality. His catholic outlook and logically straightforward approach had enabled him to cull from Italian, Dutch and French late-Renaissance sources what was best in each and fuse all the elements into a consistent whole, instinct with sturdy virility. At the same time, his adroit use of materials and his tempered interpretation of Baroque decoration supplied enrichment where it was appropriate, without falling into saccharine exuberance. This style appealed to the vigorous mentality and tastes of the period. It met the requirements of physical comfort and gave aesthetic satisfaction at the same time.

It mattered little, or not at all, to the Southern planters that Burlington and the Palladian purists were disparaging the Wren school and trying to impose a new version of architectural Classicism on the English public; their first love satisfied them and they loyally clung to it long after Burlingtonian Palladianism had become the vogue at home. They seem, indeed, to have regarded the newer fashion somewhat as a faddish display of *parvenu* taste lacking the substantial practicality of the Wren manner.

The Later Renaissance-Early Georgian manner in architecture—covering, as it did, the reigns of Charles II, James II, William and Mary, Queen Anne and part of the reign of George I in England—in America lasted well into the reign of George II, although there are occasional concessions to the newer mode in one particular here or another there. If domestic architecture in the Colonies had been solely in the hands of architects, or architect-builders, the change in all likelihood would have come sooner; but the owners of the larger houses were frequently, if not generally, their own architects. Some knowledge of architecture was deemed essential to a gentleman's education; one or more of the splendidly-published books of architectural design had place in nearly every private library worthy of the name. Acquaintance with building styles enabled the amateur architect to indicate, however roughly, the kind of structure he wished. The builder, whose job it was to translate the idea into tangible reality, could interpret his patron's rough sketch, cope with all technical and structural problems, supply all appropriate details from his pattern books, execute them with dexterity and bring the structure to creditable realisation. And the amateur architects had their own conservative preferences. An excellent instance is *Gunston Hill*, built in 1755. George Mason insisted on a structure of early type, while William Buckland (capable architect though he was), whom Mason had brought over as an indentured servant, had to confine himself to the embellishments. In some cases, the owner-architect not only conceived the structural design but meticulously measured, dictated and supervised the execution of everything, as Washington did in remodelling and enlarging *Mount Vernon*.

The example set by the Williamsburg *Palace* bore early fruit in such great plantation houses, with their layouts of dependencies, as *Kingsmill, Morattico* (probably before 1717), *Tuckahoe* (1712-30), *Marmion* (1719-35), *Scotchtown* (c. 1725), *Stratford Hall* (Pl. 10; c. 1725), *Rosewell*, obviously inspired by *Cound Hall* in Shropshire (1726), *Westover* (Pl. 14; 1726), *Corotoman* (ante 1725), *Sabine Hall* (1729), *Berkeley* (1726), *Nomini* (c. 1730), *Ampthill* (1732-50), *York Hall* (c. 1740), *Clove* (c. 1750), *Carter's Grove* (Pl. 18; 1750-3), *Wilton* (1753) or *Elsing Green* (1758).

The building impulse was no less productive in Maryland than in Virginia—witness such houses as *His Lordship's Kindness* (c. 1735) built, it is said, by the Earl of Shrewsbury for his niece and ward, Anne Talbot, at her marriage to Henry Darnall; *Kennersley* (1704-1722), *Oxon Hill* (c. 1700), *Wye Plantation* (1747), *Warburton Manor* (c. 1745), *Belair* (1746) and many others. In the Carolinas, comparable houses, such as *Brick House*, Edisto (1725), *Fenwick Hall* (1730) and *Drayton Hall* (1738), were rising during the first half of the eighteenth century.

Characteristics common amongst these houses were hipped roofs, sometimes truncated and completed with hips of flatter pitch; square-headed doorways, sometimes with overdoor lights filled with small rectangular panes; tall and often relatively narrow windows, with broad muntins—an occasional round-arched window to light a stair or give emphasis—and segmental arches above square window-heads; rather austere exteriors, occasionally relieved by rubbed and gauged brickwork for doorway and window facings, corners, panelling of wall surfaces, belt courses or aprons beneath windows; gauged and moulded brick for such features as water-tables, chimney-caps and (whenever such marks of distinguishing emphasis occurred for square-headed doorways) pediments and pilaster caps and plinths.

Within doors, features of composition were severely architectural. There was much fine panelling, sometimes in conjunction with pilasters to accent chimneybreasts, window openings, long wall spaces or to frame important arched doorways or, in company with pediments, to dignify rectangular doorways. Vigorous, well-moulded cornices between walls and ceiling, even when some of the walls were plastered, were usually of wood. Panels sometimes had arched heads, though rectangular form was usual; bolection mouldings, particularly around fireplaces, were numerous and all moulding profiles were vigorous; when such enriching incidents as pilasters were employed, their bold relief was confined to rigid Classic precedent. Above the fire-place, with its moulded marble or stone surround, the chimney-breast displayed vigorous panelled treatment; mantel-shelf and embellishment of the fireplace itself belonged to a later mode. Angle fireplaces were a good deal used, though usually in less important rooms. Well-conceived stairs, winding with two or three runs, had broad treads, low risers and handsome handrails, spindles and brackets. When there was carved enrichment, it was often reminiscent of Grinling Gibbon or even recalled some of the earlier strapwork *motifs*, as in the stair-landing fascias at *Tuckahoe* or *Rosewell*. Another significant interior feature was the occasional painted decoration on panels, as at *Morattico* or *Marmion* (Pl. 19), or *Holly Hill*. Great diversity prevailed in the ground colours for woodwork, well exemplified by the restorations at Williams-burg. The habit of monotonously painting interior woodwork white did not become common until after the middle of the eighteenth century.

Occasional concessions to the wave of neo-Palladianism current at home now and again appeared in the design of Southern plantation houses; *Stratford Hall's* high base-ment, with outside flights of steps ascending to the *piano nobile*, is a patent reflection of Burlingtonian purism. At *Drayton Hall* (1738), in South Carolina, the central two-storeyed portico (indeed, the whole elevation) clearly recalls Palladio's *Villa Cornaro* at Piombino; the interior is distinctly Early Georgian. As to plan, while the Southern planters sometimes showed preference for the old H or E scheme, in general they were not averse to adaptations or, indeed, virtual reproductions from contemporary exem-plars in England (*cf. Cound Hall* and *Rosewell*). For their dependencies, they willingly adopted the imposing symmetrical compositions advocated by the new school, but when it came to the architectural quality of their own proper dwellings, their native English conservatism triumphed. They would have none of the Burlingtonian swank, fripperies and academic ostentation. Of none of them could it be said they were indulging in the kind of thing Pope satirised, creations 'too large to hang on a watch chain, and too small to live in'.

Thus it was that the style Wren had initiated in England—that reached its flower in Queen Anne's reign—continued through the first half of the eighteenth century; *Carter's Grove*, built in 1751, 'was more Queen Anne in style than it was Mid-Georgian'. Gibbs, Sir William Chambers, the Woods of Bath and Carr of York, who accepted Palladianism with reserve, had created with skill and discrimination an architecture sympathetic with the English scheme of living; their methods met with more approbation in America than did extreme academicism. American Early Georgian, in so far as it departed from Wren's Queen Anne, was Gibbsian.

Planters less affluent than them that built the more notable plantation houses, for the most part built dwellings evolved from the earlier manner—1½-storey abodes, either one or two rooms deep—but here and there they added features derived from Early Georgian practice, often with agreeable results.

Some of the great Virginia landowners, who lived for most of the year on their widely-scattered Tidewater estates, nevertheless maintained (or built) smaller town houses in Williamsburg, whither they came for the Court Season and its gay social life. Such are the Ludwell-Paradise house (Pl. 17) and both the Blair houses (Pls. 15, 16). Of like stamp are the Wythe house (Pl. 11), *Brafferton House* and the *President's House* (Pl. 12) at William and Mary College, all of them in the Later Renaissance-Early Georgian category. Annapolis, during the Court Season, was as gay a social centre as Williamsburg, but most of the town houses kept there by Maryland's land-owning gentry were built from the middle of the eighteenth century onward and were frequently occupied for longer periods.

Virginia and Maryland church architecture of the period was inspired by Renaissance precedent, although expressed in an altogether independent manner and not greatly affected by contemporary usage in England. *Trinity Church* (1690), Dorchester County, Maryland, *Bruton Parish Church* (Pl. 13), Williamsburg (1715), and *Christ Church*, Lancaster County, Virginia (1732), kept the traditional cruciform plan but otherwise presented a Georgian aspect. Most of the other churches built before the middle of the eighteenth century were rectangular in plan and not a few of them had hipped roofs. *Bruton Church*, *Christ Church*, Chaptico (St. Mary's County), and a few others had towers but, for the most part, towers and steeples were omitted; Colonial Virginians and Marylanders, save in few instances, did not live in towns, so the churches were built at 'crossroads, in the fields or woods, where they were most convenient of access to widely scattered rural communities. The worshippers came from long miles away on horseback, in chaises or coaches, according to rank and condition. Bells served no purpose. Hence the good old custom of steeples was in abeyance.' Had Virginians and Marylanders been town dwellers, like Charlestonians, or people of the Middle Colonies and New England, they would like as not have built more churches like *St. Philip's* (Pl. 49) or *St. Michael's* in Charleston, or like those in the Middle Colonies and the North. South Carolinians, however, built many country churches not fundamentally unlike those of Maryland and Virginia.

THE MIDDLE COLONIES

IN THE MIDDLE COLONIES, the earliest instances of permanent building occur when such traces of the Jacobean manner as appear in 'Bacon's Castle' had disappeared. The older part of the *Cannon Ball House* (already mentioned) is more Swedish in character than English. Another early brick house (now in League Island Park) in the Passyunk part of Philadelphia is *Bellaire* (Pls. 4, 5, 6), built some time between 1668 and 1677. The present double-hung sash windows presumably replace earlier mullions and transoms. The house is only one room deep with a hall through the middle; the kitchen is in a separate building. Between the hall and the rooms at each side, the panelling forms the partitions; only in the attic does the panelling cease. All the woodwork is typical of the late seventeenth century, and so exceptional that one wonders how it came there. Tradition says that during the Duke of York's Government, the deputy whom Governour Sir Edmund Andros appointed 'commander and sub-collector of New York, on Delaware Bay and river' was a 'younger son sent out in military command, who embellished his dwelling with woodwork brought from England'. Did Sir Robert Carr, or did Christopher Billopp (afterwards Lord of the *Manor of Bentley* on Staten Island) once rent this house and adorn it before his recall? We shall probably never know.

One of the first references to building after Penn received the grant of Pennsylvania is in a letter Robert Turner wrote him from Philadelphia in August, 1685. (After his first visit to his Province, Penn returned to England in 1684.) Reporting on the city's material progress, Turner says:

> 'And since I built my Brick House the Foundation which was laid at thy going, which I did design after a good Manner to encourage others and that from building with Wood, it being the first, many take Example, and some that built Wooden Houses are sorry for it. Brick building is said to be as Cheap. Bricks are exceeding good and better than when I built: more Makers fallen in and Bricks cheaper. They are 16s. English per 1000, and now many brave Brick houses are going up, with good Cellars. . . . We build most Houses with Balconies.'

Gabriel Thomas, writing in 1698, said Philadelphia then contained 'above two thousand houses . . . and most of them Stately, and of Brick, generally three Stories high, after the Mode in London'. From the outset, the city was patterned after Wren's London, rebuilt after the Great Fire. There were the same penthouses above the ground floor, the same balconies, the same brick masonry, the same details of doors and windows. In his *Founding of American Civilisation*, T. J. Wertenbaker points out that the first Pennsylvanians

'came direct from England, most of them, and as a matter of course built their city in conformity with the English standards of the day. Philadelphia from the first was a Renaissance city.'

Penn's own Manor House at *Pennsbury* (Pl. 22) was started in 1683, during his first visit, and finished afterwards so that he could live there when he came back (in 1699). Utterly neglected during the eighteenth century, it had fallen into such ruinous

Fig. F. 'Slate Roof House', brick, Philadelphia. *ante* 1699

condition that Richard Penn, in 1775, pulled it down to the foundations, intending to build thereon another house, which he never did. Instructions in Penn's letters about finishing *Pennsbury* are so full and exact, down to the minutest detail, that there was ample documentary evidence whereon to base faithful re-creation when the State Historical Commission of Pennsylvania undertook that task.

One of early Philadelphia's 'brave Brick houses' was the '*Slate Roof House*' (fig. F) built on the U plan. Finished before 1699, Penn lived in it for a time as a city residence when he came back for his second visit.

While brick was the favoured material in the city, the grey stone of the neighbourhood was so plentiful that many of the country houses were built of it—*Pencoyd*

(Pl. 23), at Bala (1683), *The Ivy*, at Cheltenham (1682), *Trevose*, in Bucks (1685), *Maen Coch*, in Haverford Township (1682), *Bolton Farm*, near Bristol (1687), *Wynne-stay*, Blockley Township (1689), *Harriton*, Lower Merion (1704) and many more. All, save one, however simplified their expression, show unmistakable kinship with the Renaissance manner. Only at *Harriton* do the stair and the moulded and chamfered ceiling beams and summers recall earlier seventeenth-century usage.

Thoroughly representative of the Early Georgian mode in the Middle Colonies are such houses as *Graeme Park* (Pls. 25, 26, 27) at Horsham (1721), *Hope Lodge* (Pls. 23, 24) in the Whitemarsh Valley (1723), *Waynesborough* in Chester County (1724), or *Stenton* (Pls. 34, 35) in the Northern Liberties of Philadelphia. The design of *Hope Lodge*, a seven-bay brick house with hipped roof and massive chimneys, has been attributed to Sir Christopher Wren, a tradition with nothing to sustain it. Possibly, however, Samuel Morris may have consulted one of Wren's younger followers when he was in England, just before he returned and built his house. It is likely that he brought back the grey Scottish marble fireplace facings and the blue and white Dutch tiles, but in 1721 (when he was planning his house) it would have been folly to import either bricks or interior woodwork (as some imagine he did). Philadelphia bricks of the best quality were abundant and cheap, and skilful Philadelphia joiners were readily available. Doors and windows are taller and narrower than those of a later period and over their tops are segmental arches. Above the doors are transoms two or three lights high and four to six lights wide. A broad hall traverses the full depth of the house and opens into spacious rooms on each side. The vigorous, severely architectural quality of the interior woodwork (Pls. 23, 24) shows the same conformity as the Southern work of the Early Georgian period to the manner of Wren and his school. At *Graeme Park*—home of the ill-fated Lieutenant-Governour Sir William Keith—panelling and interior woodwork (Pl. 25) show much the same character as at *Hope Lodge*.

Stenton, a six-bay brick house with hipped roof, is 55 feet wide by 42 feet deep, a range of kitchens, offices, orangery and servants' quarters, connected by brick-paved courts and covered ways, extending backward at the north 110 feet farther. At each side of the brick-paved and panelled entrance hall with its canted corner fireplace are spacious full-panelled parlours. Beyond a central archway is the stair hall; to the right of this, the dining-room, to the left a breakfast room and a well-concealed private stair. The whole front of the upper floor is devoted to the library, a noble room with two fireplaces and windows south, east and west; it once held the

c

finest collection of books in any private library in Colonial America. In this cheerful, sunny room, James Logan, the illustrious book-loving statesman and scholar, spent most of his time in his declining years. The woodwork throughout displays the same qualities as at *Hope Lodge* and *Graeme Park*.

Distinct from the types just noted was the local farmhouse of stone or brick (fig. G), entirely without architectural pretension (probably derived from the Welsh

FIG. G. Stone Farmhouse, Pennsylvania, retaining Penthouses. Verandah added

farmhouse) showing considerable variation in form and size. It often retained the penthouse above the ground floor, brought to Philadelphia when the city was founded. The only Mediaeval feature kept by some of the brick farmhouses (conspicuously in Salem County, New Jersey) was the patterning of gable-ends with glazed headers.

The earliest public structures of this period were the *Court House* in New Castle (*ante* 1682), the little stone *Court House* at Chester, and the old *Court House* (fig. H) in Philadelphia (1707—demolished 1828); the last very like the Market Hall in an English county town. The most noteworthy structure was the *State House* (Pls. 28-33) in Philadelphia (now known as *Independence Hall*), designed by the Hon. Andrew Hamilton (Pl. 30), begun in 1732. Originally planned without a tower, the stair-tower was not started till about 1740 and the upper stage of the brickwork, with its surmounting steeple, was not finished till the middle of the century. This later date of the tower's completion probably accounts for the greater exuberance of detail in its interior woodwork.

The foremost church building was *Christ Church* (Pl. 34) in Philadelphia (reminiscent of *St. Andrew's-by-the-Wardrobe*), designed by Dr. John Kearsley and begun in

FIG. H. Old Court House, Philadelphia, Brick, 1707

1727, though the spire was not finished till just after the middle of the century when a ring of eight bells was brought from London. Among earlier churches was the *Gloria Dei* (1700) in Southwark, Philadelphia, a brick structure built by the Swedes, though now an Anglican church; naturally, it shows Swedish characteristics. *Trinity*, Oxford, Philadelphia (1711), another brick structure, apart from sporadic patterning of the walls in black headers, is a wholly Georgian small country church. *St. David's* (1715), Radnor (fig. I), and *St. Peter's-in-the-Great-Valley* (present building 1744), though their features are Early Georgian, recall some of the little churches on the Welsh Border; originally, both parishes were mainly Welsh. '*Old Swedes*', Wilmington, and '*Old Drawyer's*', 'down below' in Delaware, also deserve notice, while *Immanuel*, New Castle (c. 1700), was a good Queen Anne structure until the 'improvements' of 1820 spoiled it. Quaker meeting-houses were as plain as pipe-stems and resembled magnified brick or stone (rubble) farmhouses.

In New York, the earliest phase of our period is best represented by the oldest part of the *Philipse Manor House* (Pl. 36), at Yonkers (*ante* 1682), and *Fraunces's Tavern* (Pl. 35) in Broad Street, New York City, built during the reign of Queen Anne.

23

Fig. I. St. David's Church, Radnor, Pennsylvania. 1715

The former, a five-bay hipped-roof stone house, now forms the southern end of the building; there can be little doubt that Frederick Philipse, first Lord of the Manor, designed it himself. When built, it was a distinguished example of American domestic architecture. What is left of the original work, inside and out, coincides with contemporary characteristics noted in the South and Pennsylvania, but so many later embellishments have been added in the several modes of succeeding eras that only discriminating analysis can disentangle the work of different dates. *Fraunces's Tavern*, originally the town house of the Van Cortlandts and De Lanceys, is clearly akin to the large London house of the day, but many alterations and 'graftings' have occurred during the years of changing occupancies and uses.

The Van Cortlandt house in Van Cortlandt Park, New York City (not to be confused with the much older *Van Cortlandt Manor House*, at Croton-on-Hudson), built a little before 1750, instances the later phase of our period. A five-bay hipped-roof stone structure with brick trim, the panelling and other interior adornments display the reserve seen in other houses of the first half of the eighteenth century. One of the most striking features of exterior detail is the procession of grotesque heads or masques carved in high relief on the window keystones. They are not common in American Georgian architecture but other examples occur at *Christ Church* and the *State House*, in Philadelphia, and in the trim of some of the small circular windows in the gable-ends of the *Old State House* in Boston.

It is unfortunate that few New York Georgian houses of the first half of the eighteenth century remain; they have either been demolished or else have suffered changes that completely destroy their character. Widespread Georgian influence, however, produced a variety of hybrids—bodies of diverse provenance with grafted Georgian features. A good example is the Mandeville house (fig. J) at Garrison-on-Hudson. Built in 1735, the exterior typifies the plain local farmhouse vernacular of the period; inside, the panelling and other woodwork proclaim Queen Anne-Early Georgian usage.

Fig. J. Mandeville House, Garrison-on-Hudson, New York, 1735

NEW ENGLAND

RENAISSANCE INFLUENCE APPEARED early in New England. Whatever lingering Mediaeval features they may have retained, a number of late seventeenth-century houses showed at least some evidence of the new leaven. It may have been a hipped-roof, as at the Moody-Ridgeway house at Newbury (1658); a belt course and seg-mental arches over door and windows, as at the Peter Tufts or Cradock house (fig. K) at Medford (c. 1677); a hipped roof and ornament about the door 'constructed after the Doric order', as at the Jeremiah Wilson house in the Narragansett Country, 'forty-two feet by fifty-six' (c. 1665—demolished 1823); a straight cornice with modillions, as well as 'arrangement of mass and detail', as at the *Old Province House* in Boston (c. 1679); belt courses and segmental door and window arches, as at the

FIG. K. Tufts or Cradock house, Medford, Massachusetts. *c.* 1677

Hazen Garrison house at Haverhill (*c.* 1680); or belt courses, segmental arches and moulded cornice, as at the Durston Garrison house at Haverhill (*c.* 1697). Several of these houses were of wooden construction.

The most notable New England adjustment to Classic occasions was the wholesale grafting of the New England wooden or clapboard tradition (which by this time had become firmly fixed) upon a mode of architectural expression hitherto invariably interpreted in brick or stone in England, as it commonly was elsewhere in the American Colonies. Even when the fabric was virtually of brick, as were the Royall house at

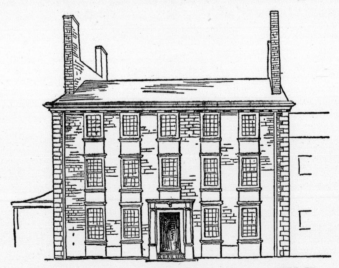

FIG. L. Royall house, Medford, Massachusetts. 1733-37

26

Medford (fig. L) and many others, it was encased in an outer shell of wood—sometimes bevelled, painted and sanded to simulate cut stone.

A marked peculiarity of New England Early Georgian houses in wood, a peculiarity perhaps invited and intensified by this choice of wood casing, is the comparative austerity and absence of embellishment from a great many exteriors, in sharp contrast with the wealth of embellishment within. Indeed, judging from the exterior, one is wholly unprepared to find exquisite interiors on entering. This shearing off or repression of outward architectural graces oftentimes makes it exceedingly difficult to tell at first glance whether a house belongs in the Georgian category or not, especially if it has suffered the obliterations incident to extensive replacements of weatherboarding; time and again, from outside, only the roofs (and they have frequently been altered) and the dimensions and placing of windows and doors now indicate generic status. Fire, too, has made havoc of many of these houses. Disastrous fires in Boston took such toll of wooden structures that further wooden building was forbidden (a prohibition not always strictly observed).

While comparatively few of the Early Georgian wooden houses have kept their pristine appearance, for the causes just noted, those that have remained intact often display external features showing close kinship with Later-Renaissance-Early-Georgian usage in England. The Dummer house at Byfield (c. 1715), the Knight-Short house at

FIG. M. Doorway, Dummer house, Byfield, Massachusetts, c. 1715

27

Newbury (1717) or the Royall house at Medford (in its present form, 1733-37) and sundry others are representative examples. Occasionally there are instances of the restrained Baroque enrichment Wren often employed with happy effect, as in the doorway of the Dummer house (fig. M), where vigorously-carved panels take the place of flanking pilasters. We find shell overdoor hoods, segmental or scroll pediments over doorways and a wealth of rich adornment in pilasters, carved capitals and well-wrought mouldings, all designed and executed in a manner reminiscent of Queen Anne's Gate or Grosvenor Road. The mouldings are bold and the torus or cushion mould frequently occurs as a frieze; well executed capitals crown flanking pilasters and sometimes imposts support an entablature. Straight transoms of small square lights are frequent. The Royall house (fig. L) exhibits a system of aprons in high relief beneath the windows of all three storeys, as well as quoins and one façade of V-channelled rustication in imitation of cut stone.

Although there was a tendency, even in New England, towards building materials more permanent than wood, a growing urge for more academic graces ran counter to it because skilful stone-cutters were few. If wood could be used for cornices and the enrichment of doorways in masonry buildings, as elsewhere, in the Colonies and in the lesser houses in England, why not use it for the whole front of a house, where the most important openings were, even though the rest of the structure were brick?

Amongst the masonry houses of the period, particular significance attaches to the Tufts house (fig. K) at Medford (c. 1677); the Marston house in Salem (brick—1707); the Hutchinson house (fig. N) in Boston (c. 1681); the McPhaedris-Warner

Fig. N. Hutchinson house, Boston, Brick with Stone Trim. c. 1681

28

house (Pl. 40) in Portsmouth, New Hampshire (*c.* 1722); and the Hancock house in Boston (1737).

When an enraged Stamp Act mob sacked Governour Hutchinson's house in 1765, an officer afterwards wrote the Lords of Trade:

> 'As for the house, which from the structure and inside finishing seemed to be from a design of Inigo Jones or his successor, it appears they were a long time resolved to level it to the ground. They worked three hours at the cupola before they could get it down, and they uncovered part of the roof; but I suppose, that the thickness of the walls, which were of very fine brickwork, adorned with Ionic [freestone] pilasters worked into the wall, prevented their completing their purpose.'

Evidence, this, not only of sound construction but also of a full flowering of the Later Renaissance at so early a date in Boston. The McPhaedris-Warner house with its roof balustrade, panelled chimneys, dormers of alternating pattern, tall windows and segmental window-arches, splendid brickwork and doorway framed by handsome pilasters and a segmental pediment, consistently displays all the Early Georgian ear-marks. In the Hancock house, built of granite ashlar with Connecticut sandstone trim,

FIG. O. 'Two-Chimney' Weatherboarded or Shingled Farmhouse, New England

the Early Georgian manner reached its climax of elaboration—doors and windows 'sumptuously framed', quoins, rustications, cornice modillions carved, roof balustrades, dormers of alternating pattern, engaged columns flanking the doorway and ornately carved brackets supporting the balcony above, while the window opening on the balcony repeated the enframement of the door underneath and was topped by a scroll pediment besides. All these houses were fully articulated in plan with convenient circulation assured. The Hancock house originally had two wings, a ball-room in one, kitchen and offices in the other.

Interiors in these and many more of their type were as consistently fine as the exteriors; there were the same richly panelled rooms with large bevel-flush panels (occasionally panels enclosed in bolection mouldings), the same robustly contoured cornice mouldings, the same pilasters, the same well-contrived stairs with handsome balusters, and the same excellent carving of capitals, stair brackets or whatever else Early Georgian genius prescribed, as noted in the Southern and Middle Colonies houses of the period. Not long after 1730 we first hear of wall-paper as a permanent interior adornment in lieu of panelling. When Thomas Hancock wrote in 1737 and ordered some for his house, he mentioned paper previously brought over, gay with 'Birds, Peacocks, Macoys, Squirrels, Monkeys, Fruit & Flowers'.

As in the Middle Colonies, there were hundreds of houses completely without attempt at architectural grace, and with no Georgian affinities. They were 'just houses',

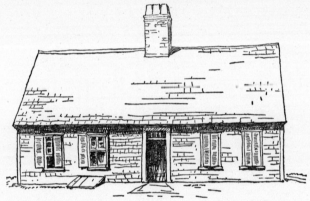

FIG. P. 'One-Chimney' or 'Salt-Box' Weatherboarded or Shingled Farmhouse, New England

weatherboarded or shingled, simple and purely utilitarian. They were prevalently of two sorts, the two-chimney type (fig. O) and the one-chimney type (fig. P) usually known as 'salt-box'.

The *Old Boston State House* (Pl. 39) is the finest example of the period's public building in New England (1713). Gable-end embellishments with the lion and the unicorn, and the balconied window, as well as every other detail of structure and adornment, inside and out, throughout its length of 110 feet, faithfully represent Later Renaissance standards. Another public structure also instinct with the same spirit is the *Old Colony House* (Pl. 36) at Newport, designed by Richard Munday—one of the few known early architects—and built in 1739. *Faneuil Hall*, Boston, built in 1741 (Pl. 47) as a market hall and place for public meetings, worthily represents New England public architecture towards the end of the era; though the spirit of the original building, designed by the painter John Smibert, was preserved, its present form dates from Bulfinch's enlargement in 1805.

Massachusetts Hall (Pl. 41) in Harvard Yard, Cambridge, built in 1720, is an outstanding instance of American college architecture for the period. *Hollis Hall* (Pl. 37) and *Harvard Hall* (Pl. 38), though not built until after the middle of the century (*Harvard* to replace an earlier namesake destroyed by fire), have nevertheless

FIG. Q. King's Chapel, Boston. 1749

preserved substantially the earlier spirit. *Massachusetts*, *Hollis*, *Harvard* and *Stoughton*, between them, give Harvard Yard much the same general atmosphere as King's Bench Walk.

In church architecture, *King's Chapel* (fig. Q), a building of carefully dressed granite ashlar, designed by Peter Harrison and built in 1749—the third structure on the site since the first *King's Chapel* for Church of England Bostonians, erected in 1688 —marks the close of the era. As it stands, *King's Chapel* is not exactly as Harrison planned it; there was to have been a steeple surmounting the tower. Severely plain without, the interior, with its rows of coupled Corinthian columns upholding the

31

galleries and supporting the roof, exhibits all the wealth of Classic embellishment one would find in London churches of the period. After the Revolution, *King's Chapel* passed to the Congregationalists and, later, to the Unitarians.

The oldest church structure now standing in Boston is *Christ Church (Old North)*. Built of brick, in 1723, for a Church of England congregation, it is still Anglican, though no longer in the Diocese of London, as were all American churches until the Revolution (after which American bishops were consecrated). The austere body and graceful spire recall Wren's labours in London and seem to have inspired many subsequent churches—some of them brick, some wooden—instinct with the Wren spirit, which arose throughout New England. In this number must be mentioned *Christ Church*, Cambridge, and *Trinity Church*, Newport (1726), the latter a wholly wooden structure. Even the *Old South*, built two years later, a brick version of the early New England wooden meeting-house, showed the influence of Peter Harrison's *Christ Church* in its spire and general architectural tone

THE PALLADIAN MID-GEORGIAN ERA

ORKINGS OF PALLADIAN leaven became clearly apparent in mid-eighteenth-century architecture in the Colonies. Conscious effort for sophisticated effect employed academic resources in both composition and the particulars of embellishment. Balance and symmetry became of prime concern. 'Outward and visible signs of an inward and spiritual' (and rationalised) Palladianism, adapted to Anglo-Saxon needs and non-Latin climate were: (1) emphasis on central pediments, often surmounting a forward offset from the façade (sometimes too shallow to be termed a 'pavilion'); (2) centralised Palladian windows (although they had already appeared at *Christ Church* and the *State House* tower in Philadelphia); (3) broader windows with larger panes and narrower muntins; (4) flat window arches with splayed bricks and oftentimes conspicuous keyblocks; (5) less stress on rubbed and gauged brickwork for colour contrast and surface ornament; (6) greater use of quoins and rustication; (7) occasional use of the *piano nobile* or, at least, a high basement; and (8) more elaborate doorways framed between pilasters or engaged columns, surmounted by pediments, the doorheads often arched and filled with fanlights. Square-headed doorways and rectangular transoms were not altogether disused, but semi-circular arches and fanlights were favoured.

Within doors, panelling was still used, but no longer of first moment for important rooms; greater expanses of plastered wall invited paint or wall-paper, of which various kinds were becoming more available. Engravings and coloured prints were more plentiful—easier to hang on plaster than on panelling. Moulded plaster cornices and ornate friezes came into fashion; decorative plasterwork enriched many ceilings. Conspicuous changes centred about the fireplace; the mantel shelf, no longer a rudimentary ledge (if that), was now fully developed atop a wooden or marble mantelpiece, often highly decorated. The wall space above invited architectural embellishment, highly articulated with pediments, consoles, entablatures, architraves, crossettes and all manner of moulded and carved enrichment. Lavish carving appeared on mould-ings wherever their contours offered opportunity.

THE SOUTH

'MOUNT AIRY' (Pl. 42), built *c.* 1758, is Virginia's earliest striking example of Palladianism. Probably designed by John Ariss (a Virginia gentleman trained in England and then practising as an architect), house and dependencies are of local brown sandstone ashlar, with trim of cut Portland and Aquia Creek stone. The main house, two storeys above a high basement, has central pedimented pavilions. A broad flight of steps between stone ramp walls leads to the entrance, within a recessed loggia with Doric pilastered piers; a low terrace, flanked by carved stone vases, raises the semi-circular forecourt above the entrance drive; quadrant passages connect two of the flanking dependencies with the main block (originally there were two other unattached forward dependencies). The pavilions are rusticated with square-sunk

FIG. R. Virginia 'Roman Country House', Palladian Type

channels; the quoins are V-sunk. Triple-arched openings of the garden-front loggia contrast with the square-headed openings of the entrance.

Waterman notes the obvious derivation of one front from *Haddo House*, Aberdeen-shire, of the other from Plate LVIII in Gibbs's *Book of Architecture*. From England came every impulse for architectural change in the Colonies; modifications were such as local requirements dictated. One requirement was scaling down designs derived from oftentimes monumental prototypes, and Waterman observes that 'the relatively small scale of Virginia Palladian is the reason for its charm and livability, and the ingenuity the designers used to attain an effect of dignity and size is a source of never-ending interest and admiration'. *Menokin*, a really small house built by the master of *Mount Airy* as a wedding gift to his daughter, is a good instance of what such adaptation could do. Built of the same stone as *Mount Airy*, with wall surfaces stuccoed except for the trim, *Menokin* with its little dependencies had all the poise of a great plantation house.

Like *Mount Airy*, many other Virginia houses built after the mid-eighteenth century evidenced Palladian principles of design, e.g. the Carlyle house in Alexandria, *Mannsfield*, *Blandfield*, *Elmwood* and the alterations and enlargements at *Mount Vernon*. Again, like *Kenmore* (c. 1752), *Gunston Hall* (1754-58), and others built a little later, there were houses whose exteriors in the earlier tradition showed occasional academic incidents while their interiors were patently Mid-Georgian.

About 1765 began to appear adaptations (fig. R) of Palladio's lesser villas. For this 'domesticated' small-scale Palladian manner—the Roman country-house style— Thomas Jefferson was probably responsible. Abandoning the large rectangular block for the main house (invariably used since the *Governour's Palace* was built), it substituted a 'group of smaller units, forming a pavilion-type house'.

FIG. S. Tulip Hill, Anne Arundel County, Maryland. 1756. West Front. Brick

In Maryland, such houses as *Montpelier* (Pl. 43), *Tulip Hill* (fig. S), *Whitehall* (Pls. 50, 51) or *Mount Clare* (Pls. 43, 44), with five-part composition (main block, symmetrical 'flankers' and connecting 'hyphen' structures) exhibited Palladian formal symmetry, besides their other unmistakable Mid-Georgian characteristics both outside and in. *Mount Clare's* colonnaded north entrance and *Tulip Hill's* west portico echo Classic precedent; *Whitehall's* garden-front 'temple' portico and the spacious hall—the full height of the house—enriched with exquisite carving and fine plasterwork, attest Governour Sharpe's support of the current vogue. In Annapolis itself, the Brice, Ridout, Scott, Paca, Chase-Lloyd houses and, beyond all others, the

Hammond-Harwood house (Pls. 51, 52), worthily exemplify the Mid-Georgian manner in Maryland. Nowhere else in America, indeed, are there finer Mid-Georgian houses than those just mentioned.

In South Carolina, the Miles Brewton house (c. 1765) built by Ezra Waite, 'civil Architect and Builder from London', of brick with a two-storey pedimented portico, both inside and out handsomely exemplifies all the academic proprieties of the era. In Charleston also, the Colonel John Stuart house (c. 1770) and the William Gibbes house (c. 1775), an engaging rendering of academicism in wood, both add to the city's Mid-Georgian repute.

Of the plaster decorations attending the gradual substitution of panelling by plastered walls (dados either wood-panelled or plastered), *Kenmore* and *Mount Vernon* offer exceptionally rich and varied examples—ceilings, cornices, friezes and (at *Kenmore*) even a chimney-piece. At *Kenmore*, writes Waterman, 'deliberately to use plaster as a finish for major rooms [in 1752] was an innovation that must have taken some courage, but its growing popularity in Georgian England must have inclined both the architect and the owners to its use.' It was, indeed, a radical departure from the earlier practice of using plaster 'only to lessen the expense of finishing unimportant rooms'. In Annapolis, too, was much excellent plasterwork. In several houses panelling, closely resembling wood, was wrought in plaster. Exceedingly rich cornices and friezes graced particularly the Hammond-Harwood and Brice houses and *Whitehall*.

Lavish carving in vigorous relief, instinct with robust Mid-Georgian spirit, gave no hint of the attenuation and flattening that came later. Oftentimes the surface of every available moulding became the vehicle for deeply-incised *motifs*—egg-and-dart, gadrooning, imbricated bands of laurel or oak, acanthus and all the related repertoire. At *Gunston Hall*, Buckland (like Chippendale) employed with deft mastery a *mélange* of Greek, Roman, Rococo and Chinese *motifs*; despite its outward aspect, *Gunston Hall's* interior was definitely Mid-Georgian. In Maryland, *Whitehall* and the Hammond-Harwood house boasted special wealth of carving; in the latter, Buckland gave free rein to his genius on overdoor and mantel embellishments, architraves of doorways and windows, the backbands of fireplace facings, skirting, chair-rails, shutters and even muntins.

In public building, the *Maryland State House* at Annapolis (1772) was representative of the era.

THE MIDDLE COLONIES

BY 1750 PHILADELPHIA had become the metropolis of the American Colonies. Much of the best domestic Georgian architecture, therefore, is to be found in the city or in its immediate neighbourhood.

While brick remained the favourite material in the city, abundance of fine local stone prompted its use for many of the country seats and we find some excellent ashlar masonry. Three of the most representative country houses of the period are *Whitby Hall* (enlargement of 1754), *Mount Pleasant* (Pls. 44, 45; 1761) and *Cliveden* (Pl. 45; *c.* 1763). *Whitby Hall* and *Cliveden* afford good ashlar examples; *Mount Pleasant's* rubble walls are stuccoed and ruled to imitate ashlar. Only in Pennsylvania were fine stone houses really common. At *Cliveden* the two subsidiary buildings are behind the main house (one of them connected later); at *Mount Pleasant*, besides the two advanced dependencies in the illustration, stable and coach-house farther forward complete the quadrangular organisation before the east front.

Plan assumed increased significance; there was considerable diversity in the ways designers secured circulation and privacy—hallways to avoid traversing one room to reach another, and secondary stairs for servants' use. *Hope Lodge* and *Stenton* had such stairs but, even after *Cliveden* (fig. T-3) was built, they continued exceptional for a long time, even in fine houses. In the Southern five-part houses, lateral passages (fig. T-1) connected with the 'flankers'; otherwise (especially in the Middle Colonies and New England) the typical Mid-Georgian house, a compact rectangular mass (two rooms deep, four rooms to a floor), had a transverse hall traversing the depth of the

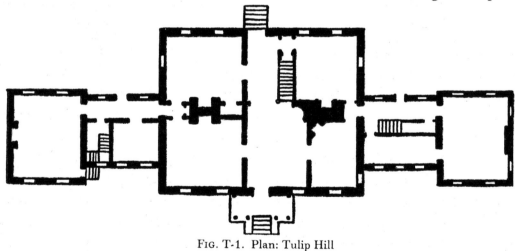

Fig. T-1. Plan: Tulip Hill

D

37

house, giving access to all rooms. This transverse hall (1) might contain the stair; the stair (2) might be in a separate compartment at the side, as at *Hope Lodge* and *Mount Pleasant* (fig. T-2); or (3) the front part of the hall might be treated as a room with the stair in a separated, smaller space to the rear, as at *Cliveden* (fig. T-3) where the front hall is separated from the stair-hall by a screen of fluted Doric columns. Whatever the hall arrangements, symmetry of space was a desideratum.

As in the South, there was a perceptible discontinuance of panelling, although the splendid ball-room (Pl. 46) of the Powel house (1765) is panelled. Ornate plaster embellishment increased, as at *Mount Pleasant* and *Belmont*, or at the Powel and Blackwell houses in the city.

Plain country farmhouses remained much as formerly save that penthouses tended to disappear as the century advanced.

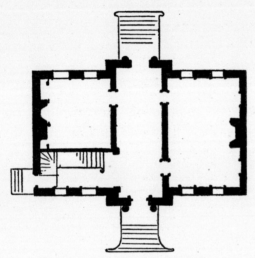

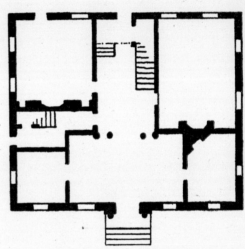

FIG. T-2. Plan: Mount Pleasant   FIG. T-3. Plan: Cliveden

In New York, *The Pastures* (Pl. 40) at Albany (1761), the Ludlow house (Pl. 41) at Claverack (1786) and *Mount Morris* (known also as the 'Jumel Mansion'; 1765) in New York City are typical. Built of wood, *Mount Morris* has quoins and a pedimented 'temple' portico with columns the full two storeys in height. Both *Mount Morris* and *The Pastures*, with roof balustrades at the eaves, show a fashion coming into favour. Although the north parlour at *The Pastures* is panelled, wall-paper is important in interior embellishment, as it also is at *Mount Morris*. At *The Pastures*, in the broad hall, and in the great gallery above it on the upper floor, the walls are covered with scenic wall-paper. The Ludlow house, though later in date, is insistently Mid-Georgian.

38

In public building, the old wing of the *Pennsylvania Hospital* (1755) followed early precedent, and this was largely true of other public structures of the period; *Carpenters' Hall* (1773) is about the only public building of fully Mid-Georgian characteristics except (much earlier) *Nassau Hall* (1742) at Princeton.

The finest ecclesiastical edifice was *St. Paul's Chapel* (1764) in New York, a chapel of ease in *Trinity Parish*, designed by James McBean, a Scot, said to have been a pupil of Gibbs. This seems likely; the handsome spire is distinctly Gibbsian. In Philadelphia, *St. Peter's Church* (1761), with its great Palladian east window, and *Zion* (1766) German Lutheran church, represent the period's church architecture.

NEW ENGLAND

OF NEW ENGLAND interpretation of Mid-Georgian Palladian proprieties in wood, there could be no better instance than the Lee house (Pl. 54) at Marblehead, Massachusetts (1768). It might be called a *bas relief* of rationalised, popularised Palladianism. The Vassall (Longfellow) house (1759) at Cambridge, another wood-encased dwelling, exhibits its Palladianism by its roof balustrade, pedimented central pavilion and four 'colossal' façade pilasters. The *Lindens* (1754) at Danvers (now removed to Washington City), with quoins, rustications and 'colossal' engaged Corinthian colums supporting the central pediment; the Lady Pepperrell house (1760) Kittery Point, Maine; the Moffat-Ladd house (1763) and the Colonel John Wentworth house (1770), Portsmouth, New Hampshire; the Hamilton house, South Berwick, Maine—these, and many more throughout New England, are typical of Mid-Georgian academicism in wood. Such brick houses as were built commonly showed the same characteristics. The Joseph Brown house (Pl. 53; 1774) in Providence, its gable-end treated as an ogee pediment, was a whimsical exception.

Although plastered walls and wall-paper (block-printed or hand-painted) were steadily winning favour, there was, nevertheless, a tendency still to rely on panelling, often with carving, as in the Lee house banquetting-room where fireplace trim, mantel and overmantel display foliated consoles and scrolls, acanthus brackets, festoons and pendants of fruit and flowers in high relief, after a design from Swan's *British Architect*. At the same time, earlier features of panelling were often retained; at the Lee house and *The Lindens* bolection mouldings appear. Another occasional item, notably at *The Lindens*, was foliated and floriated scrollwork stencilled in paint on the floor boards for borders.

D2

39

Two good brick examples of public building are the *Holden Chapel* (Pl. 53; 1754) in Harvard Yard and Newport's *Market Hall* (Pl. 47; 1761), the latter designed by Peter Harrison, apparently adapted from an elevation for *Old Somerset House* in *Vitruvius Britannicus*. Another of Harrison's buildings, Newport's *Redwood Library*, though built earlier (1749) and translated into wood with rusticated walls, Lord Burlington himself would have acclaimed. It is one of the first buildings (if not the *first*) in the Colonies with the pedimented portico of the Classic temple as the basis of design.

Noteworthy in church architecture was Joseph Brown's *First Baptist Meeting House* at Providence (Pl. 48; 1775), its spire intentionally an almost exact copy of one of Gibbs's rejected designs for *St. Martin-in-the-Fields* (Plate XXV, centre spire, *Book of Architecture*). Built of wood and painted white, the rest of the exterior does not vividly recall Gibbs's work, but the interior does. How enduring and widespread was this ecclesiastical type in the Colonies is evident on comparison with *St. Philip's* spire (Pl. 49) in Charleston (1718), built more than half a century earlier.

LATE GEORGIAN NEO-CLASSICISM

LATE GEORGIAN NEO-CLASSICISM—the manner of the Adelphi—counted but little until after the Revolutionary War. Partly because of Colonial conservatism, the Mid-Georgian mode had continued to dominate building design up to the outbreak of hostilities. During the war, there was little building.

At the return of peace (1783), many of the wealthy Loyalists had left the country, many of the formerly wealthy supporters of independence were now impoverished or, indeed, ruined. Nevertheless, despite the disunity and jealousies amongst the now independent States, trade gradually revived and the closing years of the eighteenth century saw marked prosperity. With renewed prosperity came the urge towards expansion and fresh impetus to build. People were ready for something new. Enthusiasm for Classic precedent was in the very air.

At the same time, there was little popular reverence for the architectural work of earlier years. Many Classic enthusiasts, yeasty and more vocal than the old well-to-do conservative element, denounced Early and Mid-Georgian structures as old-fashioned, barbarous, crude. Sharing this contempt for pre-Revolutionary work, Thomas Jefferson, in 1784, called the William and Mary College buildings 'rude misshapen piles, which, but that they have roofs, would be taken for brick kilns'. Equally contemptuous of building in England, in 1786 he wrote, 'Their architecture is in the most wretched style I ever saw, not meaning to except America, where it is bad, or even Virginia, where it is worse than in any other part of America, that I have seen.' (In 1779 he had drawn plans for remodelling the *Governour's Palace* at Williamsburg, fortunately never carried out.)

Notwithstanding Jefferson's low opinion of English architecture, his manifest leaning towards French ideals and his zeal for close adherence to Palladian precept, outside of his immediate sphere of personal influence, America still relied mainly upon British architectural guidance, used British architectural books and assimilated the practices of the Brothers Adam and their imitators, in composition, plan and embellishment.

While Mid-Georgian exponents regarded the whole exterior as a subject for symmetrically balanced composition, with due decorative emphasis, the Adam school, valuing no less the effect of the whole building in both proportion and detail, also stressed their conviction that

> 'Classic precedents were susceptible of a far wider and more elastic interpretation than had hitherto been given them, that architecture and the decorative arts in the golden ages of Greek and Roman development had not been straitly confined by an unalterably rigid set of rules and . . . conventions whose authoritative exposition was to be found only in the works of Vitruvius, Vignola and the other dogmatists . . . and that Classicism, without being adulterated or distorted and robbed of its fundamental genius, was susceptible of a previously undreamed of urbanity, refinement and even playful exuberance of expression.'

The attentuation and slender grace, the lively, diversified system of decorative *motifs* (all derived, however, from Classic precedent), and the geniality of the new fashion met ready welcome in America.

Neo-Classicism served as an architectural laxative. General lightening and enlivenment of exteriors ensued upon the use of wrought iron for balconies and other incidentals; delicate leaded tracery in semi-circular or elliptical fanlights and in the narrow sidelights that now appeared at the sides of doors; graceful urns atop pediments, at roof-corners, or at intervals on roof balustrades; arched countersunk panels framing important doorways or windows to produce a play of light and shadow, or panels of varied shapes on plain wall surfaces to give diversity of planes; and a more subtle employment of stucco, either for contrast or as a foil to some single enriching incident. While semi-octagon ends had previously appeared on wings, semi-octagon, semi-elliptical and semi-circular projections from the main mass now became frequent features of design. Attenuation appeared both in the proportions of columns, colonnettes, pilasters and the contours of mouldings, and also in the outlines of decorative *motifs*. At the same time, there was noticeable suppression of eaves and other external projections. Windows quite generally increased in size, with larger panes and thin muntins. 'Roman' semi-circular windows and small windows, circular, oval or octagonal lent variety.

In plan, there were varied room-shapes—round, semi-circular, octagonal, elliptical; and there were rooms with semi-circular, arc-shaped, tribune or arcaded ends to enhance elegance, vivacity or interest. Winding stairs, circular or elliptical on plan, also appeared.

The ascendancy of plaster walls indoors opened the way to all the possibilities of compo decoration. Both in plaster and compo the decorations were refined in scale and in low relief—oval fans, water-leaf paterae, spandril fans, Classic urns and lamps, griffins, medallions, garlands, drops and swags of husks and ball-flowers, fluting and quilling, masques, mythological and Classic figures, anthemia and all the graceful inventions of Pompeian arabesques. All interior projections were minimised so as to assist sense of spaciousness. 'Continued chimney pieces' were no longer fashionable; a plain wall surface above the mantel made an effective foil for decoration lavished on the mantel itself.

There were definitely two general types of houses—those in which both exterior and interior were patently in the new mode, and those in which Neo-Classicism was merely a manner of interior decoration while outwardly they adhered to earlier usage.

THE SOUTH

THE DEMOCRATISED TYPE of Palladianism based on Palladio's 'Roman Country House' style (fig. R), retained considerable popularity throughout the century and later. Nevertheless, the Adam impulse was plainly manifest in such houses as *Dumbarton House* (Pls. 55, 56) in Georgetown and *Homewood* (Pls. 57, 58) in Baltimore, with many more to keep them company. In Charleston, the Manigault house (*c.* 1790), a three-storey hipped-roof brick structure with suppressed external projections; a high basement and a two-storey portico in front; a large central 'Roman' window in the upper storey; a dining-room ending in a semi-circular bay; and a circular stair set in another semi-circular bay opposite the entrance, both externally and internally gave clear evidence of its derivation. The Manigault house was by no means alone in the Carolinas. In Washington City the *White House* (President's House), designed by Hoban in 1792, is said to have been inspired by the Duke of Leinster's Dublin house. And there was the *Octagon House*, designed by Dr. Thornton.

This era's public building embraced the *Virginia Capitol* in Richmond (patterned after the *Maison Carrée* at Nîmes, by Jefferson and Clérisseau), Jefferson's Palladian work at the University of Virginia, and the contentious beginnings of the *Capitol* in Washington City.

THE MIDDLE STATES

IN PHILADELPHIA, William Hamilton's enlargement and remodelling (1788) left *The Woodlands* (Pl. 56, fig. T-4) a house in good Adam manner. The circular vestibule has a saucer-dome ceiling supported by eight columns with waterleaf capitals, and arched niches between the four door arches. The larger bedrooms have bed alcoves. John Penn's *Solitude* (1784) has exquisite ceiling decorations and a handsome wrought-iron stair balustrade. William Bingham's Philadelphia house (fig. U; *ante* 1788), with its

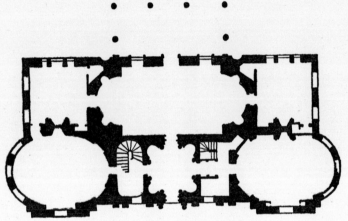

FIG. T-4. Plan: The Woodlands

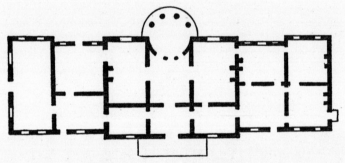

FIG. T-5. Plan: Tudor Place

marble stair and corresponding appointments—Bulfinch considered it much too handsome a house for any American—both inside and out as representative an 'Adam' creation as one could wish, was reputedly inspired by the Duke of Manchester's London house. The *President's House* (fig. V) in Philadelphia, *Lemon Hill, Upsala, The Highlands* at the edge of the Whitemarsh Valley, the Read house in New Castle and sundry others all belong in the 'Adam' category. In New York, such domestic examples as the *'House of History'*, at Kinderhook, and many others in both brick and wood, witness the wide diffusion of the Neo-Classic manner.

Of public structures there could be no more apposite instances than the building of the *Library Company of Philadelphia* (fig. W; 1790) and the central block of the

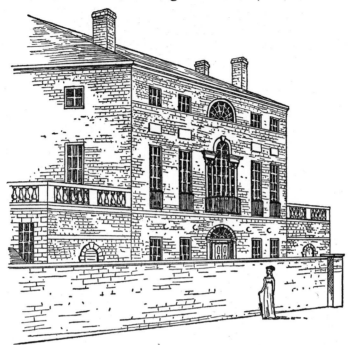

FIG. U. William Bingham's Philadelphia house. *ante* 1788. Brick

FIG. V. President's House, Philadelphia. 1792. Brick

45

FIG. W. Library Company of Philadelphia. 1790. Brick. Designed by Dr. Thornton

Pennsylvania Hospital (Pl. 57; 1796-1804). In New York City, in 1789 L'Enfant re-modelled the old *Federal Hall*, and *Government House* was made ready for Washington's residence. McComb's comely (New York) *City Hall*, though not finished until 1812, was one of the most ambitious undertakings attributable to the Neo-Classic spirit of the age; Mangin's French influence was also perceptible.

NEW ENGLAND

THE NAMES OF Charles Bulfinch, of Boston, and Samuel McIntire, of Salem, are inseparably associated with this era's New England architecture. The freshness, delicacy and slender elegance of the Adam manner claimed their adherence; they, and those who followed their lead, enriched the countryside with a wealth of archi-tecture—domestic, public and ecclesiastical—that now forms a priceless (and appre-ciated) heritage of New Englanders. Though much remains, it is matter of deep regret that some of Bulfinch's choicest work in Boston was long ago demolished before the march of commercialism. His Harrison Gray Otis house (Pl. 60; *c.* 1795) in Cam-bridge Street, and the two other Boston houses he designed afterwards for the same gentleman, show his skilful, reserved use of precedent.

A peculiarly New England development of the period was the square three-storey house, of which the Pingree house (Pl. 60) in Salem, designed by McIntire, is typical. The three-storey 'square' with virtually flat roof (often surrounded by eaves balustrades) is to be found throughout New England. Many of the best for which McIntire was responsible, in or near Salem, are replete with the exquisite carving he delighted to lavish on his interiors. Occasionally these 'squares', if reticent externally, nevertheless disclose unexpected enrichment within.

Of the many similar New England wooden houses, the house (Pl. 59; c. 1798) at Portsmouth, New Hampshire, is a felicitous illustration. At Orford, New Hampshire (quite on the opposite side of the State) a group of wooden houses, one by Bulfinch and four by his emulators, make a visit to that village a genuine delight.

The outstanding public building was Bulfinch's *Massachusetts State House* (Pl. 61; 1795), its gilded dome crowning Beacon Hill, deservedly the pride of Boston and object of affectionate admiration to all of Massachusetts. Nor should his earlier *Connecticut State House* at Hartford be overlooked. Another significant structure was the *Massachusetts General Hospital*, also by Bulfinch.

This era saw the building of many of the seemly churches (not a few of them successors of earlier structures) that dominate the greens of New England villages. Of them all, none is more instinct with tempered Neo-Classic spirit than Bulfinch's *Unitarian Church* (Pl. 63) at Lancaster. *St. Stephen's Roman Catholic Church* in Boston, and the *Park Street Church*, designed by Peter Banner, are typical of urban church architecture.

THE GRAECO-ROMAN REGENCY
('FEDERAL') MANNER

THE GRAECO-ROMAN REGENCY or 'Federal' manner was fundamentally Adam Neo-Classicism reduced to its lowest terms and streamlined, plus a moderate admixture of purely Greek derivation. In England, Henry Holland, cloyed by excess of 'confectionery' (into which the Adam manner was degenerating), started a revolt against over-elaboration when he designed *Southill* (1795) in Bedfordshire. Others followed his lead and the reaction reached its full flowering under the Regency, whence the style took its name. In America, Bulfinch had always eschewed the superficial frivolities of Neo-Classicism; to exercise restraint accorded with his genius. Latrobe, fresh from current developments in England and tutelage under Cockerell and Smeaton, practised the gospel of suave austerity directly upon his arrival in America. He was soon ably supported by his pupil Robert Mills; Dr. Thornton followed in his wake a little later.

In America, as in England, there were the same four-centred arches; walls with blind arcades, the tops of the countersunk panels circular, four-centred or else segmental curves cut short at their junction with the verticals; 'Wyatt' or three-part windows in place of Palladian windows; arched or square-headed windows within countersunk arched panels; eaves and cornices much repressed or replaced by parapets; great delicacy and tenuity of mouldings; sashes with $\frac{5}{8}''$ muntins; and greater use of stucco, often for whole exteriors or, in lieu of stucco, masonry painted. Exponents of the Regency or 'Federal' manner still felt free to combine Roman arch and curvilinear grace with Greek purity of line. They had not yet become convinced that curving lines were accursed and that architectural orthodoxy lay only in the grim rectilinear intransigeance of the subsequent Greek Revival. (The out-and-out Greek Revival often produced sheer brutal clumsiness.)

48

THE SOUTH

THE MOST TYPICAL and illuminating piece of Regency domestic architecture is *Tudor Place* (Pl. 64, fig. T-5) in Georgetown, finished by Dr. Thornton in 1816. By that time he must have seen, or heard of, *Gore House* (Pl. 61) at Waltham (he had already designed the *Octagon House*, indicative of his changing attitude). The illustrations are sufficiently convincing; the interior fulfills exterior promise. The Wickham house (now the *Valentine Museum*) and the Archer house in Richmond, designed by Mills, are in typical Regency manner, likewise the Scarborough and Telfair houses in Savannah, designed by William Jay ('architect and surveyor'), to say nothing of numerous other examples in the South.

In public building, Dr. Thornton's original design for the *Capitol* in Washington City, with its *Pantheon*-like saucer dome, seems to have foreshadowed incipient Regency leanings. Also to this era belong Mills's *Court House* in Richmond, his *Record Office* in Charleston, *South Carolina State Insane Asylum*, and Camden *Court House*. His finest public work in the South is the *Washington Monument* in Baltimore, begun in 1815.

Latrobe's *St. John's Church* in Washington City is scarcely representative because of sundry later alterations, but his justly-celebrated *Basilica of the Assumption of the Blessed Virgin Mary* (the Roman Catholic Cathedral) in Baltimore is a most convincing monumental instance of definitely Regency architecture—a large, present *fact*, uncomfortable-to-digest and awkward-to-explain for them that like to ignore the Regency manner's existence and take a kangaroo leap straight from Adamesque

FIG. X. Waln House, Philadelphia. Designed by Latrobe. Brick

49

urbanities to the Greek Revival's stark rigidities without reckoning any intervening transitional phase.

THE MIDDLE STATES

LATROBE'S DOMESTIC WORK in Philadelphia long ago disappeared, but fortunately we have old sketches of the Waln (fig. X), Burd and other houses whose close kinship to contemporary Regency houses in England is unmistakable. Of Mills's domestic work only a forlorn remnant is left. A thoroughly amiable small Regency example (architect unknown) is *Swanwick* (fig. Y) at Farnhurst by New Castle. The curious embellishment of the belt course consists of small iron inserts in the stucco; their succession creates a running key-fret pattern. Regency 'Gothick' also appeared. Latrobe built *Sedgeley*, a country-seat; likewise a 'Gothick' bank!

FIG. Y. Swanwick, Farnhurst by New Castle, Delaware. c. 1820. Stucco

Public building of the era in Philadelphian has fared almost as ill as domestic— nearly all demolished. In 1798 Latrobe designed his white marble *Bank of Pennsylvania*, certainly not devoid of 'Roman' curves (as his elevations, sections and plans abundantly prove). Illustrations of another of his buildings, *Centre Square Pumping Station* (Pl. 62) speak for themselves. Mills's *Pennsylvania State Capitol* at Harrisburg, and Strickland's rebuilding of the '*New Theatre*' (1820) in Philadelphia (so called to distinguish it from the *old* theatre in Southwark), were both admirable instances of Regency manner. One of the best things Mills did in Philadelphia was the *Upper Ferry Bridge* (1809-12) over the Schuylkill, a graceful covered structure spanning the river with one elliptical arch of 340 feet (burned in 1818). His Burlington (New Jersey) *Gaol* (1808) still displays its austere grace. Most of John Haviland's creations, including his merry Chinese pagoda and casino for the *Pagoda and Labyrinth Garden*, have disappeared; however, his *Deaf and Dumb Asylum* (now the *Philadelphia Museum of Art's*

School of Industrial Arts) and the old building of the *Franklin Institute* (now the *Atwater Kent Museum*) still survive. Also, still representing the era are the *Old Fairmount Water Works* (frontispiece; 1822); the design is accredited to an engineer formerly in Latrobe's office. Of whence came the inspiration, there can be little doubt.

While living in Philadelphia, Mills initiated the auditorium type of structure for evangelical congregations when he built '*Round Top*' (1808), the *First Baptist Church*, a large circular edifice with a dome. A few years later he built the octagonal *Unitarian Church*, a seemly Regency structure, if we may judge from old engravings. *St. Stephen's Church*, with its twin 'pepper-box' towers, designed by William Strickland, is witness to the 'Gothick' fad of the period.

NEW ENGLAND

GORE HOUSE (Pl. 61; *c.* 1805) at Waltham, Massachusetts, is popularly attributed to Charles Bulfinch. Whether he designed it (as seems most likely) or not, it is an impressive evidence of New England's ready adoption of Regency ideals. Bulfinch's second Harrison Gray Otis house, on Mount Vernon Street in Boston, with its arcaded front and iron balconies would be quite as much in place in Papworth's Regency Cheltenham as where it stands on American soil. The same might be said of many other houses by Bulfinch or his imitators, both in Boston and elsewhere.

Besides the *Massachusetts State Prison* at Charlestown (1803) and the Boston *Court House* (later *City Hall*—1810), Bulfinch's public work included court houses for the counties of Norfolk, Suffolk, Worcester, Middlesex and Essex. One of his most important public commissions at this time (1805) was the enlargement of *Faneuil Hall* (Pl. 47), when he widened the building to its present seven bays and added the top floor with its Ionic pilasters. Schools, customs-houses, state-houses and other public structures by Bulfinch or those who worked in the spirit of this period are to be found in sundry places throughout New England.

Two Boston churches designed by Asher Benjamin—the *Charles Street Church* and the *West Church*—both show streamlined qualities conformable to Regency practice. Like some of Bulfinch's churches (e.g. at Lancaster (Pl. 63; 1816) or *St. Stephen's Roman Catholic Church* in Boston), it is a little puzzling whether to call them chastened products of Adamesque Neo-Classic freedom or—what really amounts to the same thing—embodiments of the Regency spirit. Not all New England churches of the era were of this genus. There were occasional excursions into Regency 'Gothick.' Bulfinch himself made one (the *Federal Street Church*, 1809); further essays he wisely forbore.

The 'Gothick taste'—anomalous by-product of the Regency era—evoked a few agreeable though capricious dwellings (mostly of the cottage type) in both England and America, and also a seemly species of hall-lanthorn but, when applied to church design, the results at best were unhappy. Providence (Rhode Island) has several churches in the 'Gothick taste' and so have some other places in New England. The most that can be said for these pseudo-Gothic whimsies is that they were ingenious. Fortunately for posterity, most of the architectural ingenuity of the period was otherwise applied.

ARCHITECTS, BUILDERS AND BOOKS

UNTIL NEARLY THE end of the eighteenth century, America lacked professional architects—professionals in the present sense of the term, technically trained in every respect, and receiving the customary emoluments of their calling. Those who had previously practised architecture fell short of the modern definition in one way or another. Even men like John Ariss, in Virginia (the extent of whose actual training is conjectural); Ezra Waite, in Charleston, advertised as 'Civil Architect, House-Builder in general and Carver from London'; William Buckland, in Maryland, with exceptionally meritorious achievements to his credit; McBean, in New York, reputed to have been a pupil of Gibbs; or Richard Munday and Peter Harrison, in New England, by to-day's reckoning would all fail of professional status. While Fiske Kimball freely concedes that 'Bulfinch became a professional in the nature and extent of his practice, if not in training', many of the present brotherhood would accord him this title only with grudging reservation. Thomas Jefferson, however technically competent he may have been, would now be ranked as a skilful amateur, since he seems neither to have asked nor accepted fees for his architectural labours. Dr. Thornton, notwithstanding the extent and importance of his work, was undeniably an amateur by modern standards.

Albeit we deny them the title of 'architect'—thanks to the current obsession for exactitude of labels and classifications, and our mania for specialisation—the goodly company of eighteenth-century *designers* nonetheless accomplished substantial, satisfying results that richly deserve the admiration and plaudits of posterity. Gratitude and praise are due not only them that had the vision or imagination to conceive the structures—public, ecclesiastical or domestic—but also the master-builders or 'house-wrights' that gave the structures tangible form. How significant an element were the master-builders in the life of a community is evident from the formation of the Carpenters' Company of Philadelphia, in 1724, patterned after The Worshipful

53

Company of Carpenters of London. Its purpose was to regulate the building trade and foster the best workmanship; also, there were a livery company's fraternal and beneficial provisions. Ten of the most representative and substantial master-builders were the founders, and all during the Colonial and early Federal periods the ablest men were members. The Company is still active and Carpenters' Hall houses a fine architectural library.

Attention has already been called to the fact that some knowledge of architecture was considered an essential part of a gentleman's education; 'Architecture Taught' appears in the advertisements of fashionable teachers of painting and drawing. With the aid of books, 'a cultivated owner or an ambitious mechanic was often able to erect buildings which would have honoured an architect by profession.' But in spite of the general dependence on books, there was little slavish copying. While it is sometimes possible to identify the exact source from which a given feature is taken, the eclectic process usually followed often produced a refreshing variety of legitimate combinations and consistent composition.

The owner-originators, who envisioned the general design of the buildings, may rarely have given a finished drawing, as did Thomas Jefferson, or (more likely) may have furnished only a crude draught, as did Andrew Hamilton for the *State House* in Philadelphia. This indication, usually a rudimentary thing, it was the master-builder's job to translate into three-dimensional reality. The master-builders or housewrights were nearly all both well-trained in their craft and resourceful and, for their immediate guidance, had one or more of the numerous eighteenth-century architectural pattern books, which reached the Colonies within a relatively short time of their publication in England.

With the few crude drawings made, or often none at all, the building process necessitated close collaboration between owner and builder, constant superintendence and frequent devisement 'on the job' of many a feature for which full-sized blueprints and specifications would now be prepared in advance. It is matter of record how William Penn ordered the minutest details during the building of *Pennsbury*; how Judge Hamilton was constantly obliged to settle puzzling problems of construction while the *State House* in Philadelphia was a-building; how Thomas Jefferson was ready with some ingenious solution for every difficulty that arose; or how General Washington directed every step of the remodelling of *Mount Vernon*. On the other hand, there is no doubt that the housewright alone contrived and built many a small or unimportant building without any active intervention by the owner.

Some of the books, on which 'amateur' designers and housewrights alike relied, include William Adam's *Vitruvius Scoticus*, James Gibbs's *Book of Architecture*, Colin Campbell's *Vitruvius Britannicus* and Giacomo Leoni's *Palladio*, amongst the larger and more costly tomes (not a few of which were in private libraries); and, amongst the less expensive publications of wider circulation, the various titles that appeared under the names of Robert Morris, Abraham Swan, William Halfpenny, Batty Langley, William Pain and William Salmon. Swan's *Carpenter's Complete Instructor* we know was in Buckland's library. Swan's *British Architect* (1745) was so popular in America that, in 1775, Robert Bell, 'Bookseller, Third Street next Door to St. Paul's Church' in Philadelphia, issued a pirated edition; its list of 'Encouragers' gives the names of 60 master-builders and 110 house carpenters. Under the title of *The Practical House Carpenter or Youth's Instructor*, Pain's *Practical Builder* was published in Boston in 1796, in Philadelphia in 1797. Prior to 1804, no less than four of his works were republished in America. The books just mentioned by no means exhaust the list; some of the earlier builders doubtless had Joseph Moxon's books.

There were American books, too, such as Asher Benjamin's *Country Builder's Assistant* and *American Builder's Companion*, or Owen Biddle's *Young Carpenter's Assistant*.

The names of *all* who wrought well and faithfully in the American architectural field we probably never shall know. Of the many near-architects, amateur designers and master-builders, who gave America most of its Georgian architecture, whose names we do know, it is impossible here to do more than mention a few to whom posterity is signally indebted—in the South, Henry Cary, Richard Taliaferro, John Ariss, David Minitree, John Hawks, Ezra Waite, Gabriel Manigault, William Buckland, Thomas Jefferson and General Washington; in the Middle Colonies, James Porteus (said to have come at Penn's instance), Andrew Hamilton, Dr. John Kearsley, Edmund Woolley, Ebenezer Tomlinson, John Harrison, Robert Smith, Samuel Rhoads, James McBean, John McComb, Dr. William Thornton and, for the region round about Claverack and Hudson, Barnabas Waterman; while in New England, the repute of Peter Banner, Richard Munday, Peter Harrison, John Smibert, Joseph Brown and Asher Benjamin is eclipsed only by the lustre attaching to the names of Samuel McIntire and Charles Bulfinch, the last of whom only a pettifogging technicality can exclude from the rank of 'professionals'.

When at last professional architects—indubitably professional by modern reckoning—did begin to practise, they were in a difficult position. The general public, long

55

accustomed to profit by the good nature of the gifted amateur or depend upon the competency of the master-builder, were inclined to regard the professional architect as an 'unnecessary luxury'; only by slow degrees did they accommodate themselves to the new order and become reconciled to even a fairly decent compensation for professional services. 'Even Latrobe, it is said, did not make a financial success of his profession of architecture.' As a matter of fact, his chief support seems to have come from his engineering work.

The roster of professionals in the late eighteenth and early nineteenth centuries is not long. Those who wrought, while any semblance of the Georgian spirit still remained, include Benjamin Henry Latrobe, James Hoban, Stephen Hallet, Robert Mills, William Strickland and John Haviland. Both Mills and Strickland were Latrobe's pupils; most of Strickland's work belonged to the purely Greek Revival phase of architecture, when a great many Americans were pleased to fancy themselves the spiritual and political heirs of the ancient Greeks and were sympathetically enthused by the struggle for Greek independence.

PLATES

(*Top*) ST. LUKE'S CHURCH, Isle of Wight County, Virginia. 1632

(*Bottom*) The same, from South-east

I

(*Top*) ADAM THOROUGHGOOD HOUSE, Princess Anne County, Virginia. *ante* 1644

(*Bottom*) 'BACON'S CASTLE', Surry County, Virginia. c. 1655. North Front

(*Top*) 'BACON'S CASTLE', Surry County, Virginia. c. 1655. West End
(*Bottom*) OLD STATE HOUSE, St. Mary's City, Maryland. 1676. Interior. (A Re-creation)

(*Top*) BELLAIRE, Passyunk, Philadelphia. c. 1672. South-west Front

(*Bottom*) OLD STATE HOUSE, St. Mary's City, Maryland. 1676. East Front. (A Re-creation)

4

(*Top*) BELLAIRE, Passyunk, Philadelphia. c. 1672. Stair

(*Bottom*) BACHELOR'S HOPE, St. Mary's County, Maryland. 1679. South Front

(Top) BELLAIRE, Passyunk, Philadelphia. c. 1672. Parlour

(Bottom) FORT CRAILO, Rensselaer, New York. 1642. West Front

6

(*Top*) PIETER BRONCK HOUSE, West Coxsackie, New York. 1666. Older Part of East Front

(*Bottom*) JAN HASBROUCK HOUSE, New Paltz, New York. Beginning of 18th Century

(*Top*) PARSON CAPEN HOUSE, Topsfield, Massachusetts. c. 1685

(*Bottom*) 'HOUSE OF SEVEN GABLES', Salem, Massachusetts. c. 1669

(*Top*) WREN BUILDING, WILLIAM AND MARY COLLEGE, Williamsburg, Virginia. 1695. East Front

(*Bottom*) The same, West Front. (Much restored to mid-eighteenth century aspect)

9

(*Top*) STRATFORD HALL, Westmoreland County, Virginia. c. 1725

(*Bottom*) THE CAPITOL, Williamsburg, Virginia. 1704. West Front. (A Re-creation)

(*Top*) GOVERNOUR'S PALACE, Williamsburg, Virginia. 1706. South Front (A Re-creation)

(*Bottom*) WYTHE HOUSE, Williamsburg, Virginia. c. 1755

PRESIDENT'S HOUSE, WILLIAM AND MARY COLLEGE, Williamsburg, Virginia. C. 1732. (Designed to accord with *Brafferton House*, opposite, C. 1704.)

12

BRUTON PARISH CHURCH, Williamsburg, Virginia. 1715. From South-east

WESTOVER, Charles City County, Virginia. 1726. South Front. (Connecting wings later)

14

BLAIR (wooden) HOUSE, Williamsburg, Virginia. c. 1760

BLAIR (brick) HOUSE, Williamsburg, Virginia. c. 1730. South Front

LUDWELL-PARADISE HOUSE, Williamsburg, Virginia. C. 1717. South Front

(*Top*) CARTER'S GROVE, James City County, Virginia. 1751

(*Bottom*) HOLLY HILL, Anne Arundel County, Maryland. c. 1690. East Front of Older Part

18

MARMION, King George County, Virginia. *ante 1735*. Panel Paintings c. 1770. Panelling now in *Metropolitan Museum of Art*, New York City

HIS LORDSHIP'S KINDNESS, Prince George's County, Maryland. c. 1735. East Front

HIS LORDSHIP'S KINDNESS, Prince George's County, Maryland. c. 1735. West Front

(*Top*) PENNSBURY MANOR HOUSE, Pennsylvania. Begun 1683. South Front. (A Re-creation)

(*Bottom*) KENNERSLEY, Queen Anne's County, Maryland. 1704. East Front

22

(*Top*) HOPE LODGE, Whitemarsh, Pennsylvania. 1723. The Hall

(*Bottom*) PENCOYD, Bala, Pennsylvania. 1683. South Front

HOPE LODGE, Whitemarsh, Pennsylvania. 1723. Looking across Hall

24

GRAEME PARK, Horsham, Pennsylvania. 1721. Great Parlour

GRAEME PARK, Horsham, Pennsylvania. 1721. South Front

26

GRAEME PARK, Horsham, Pennsylvania. 1721. North Front.

STATE HOUSE (INDEPENDENCE HALL), Philadelphia. 1732. North Front

28

STATE HOUSE (INDEPENDENCE HALL), Philadelphia. 1732. South Front. Tower added c. 1741. Steeple reconstructed 1828

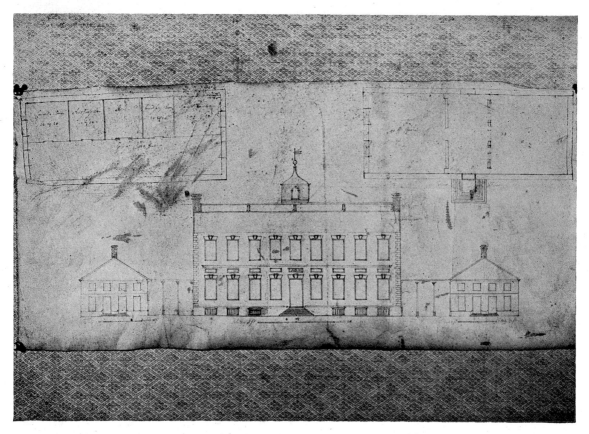

STATE HOUSE (INDEPENDENCE HALL), Philadelphia. 1732. Hon. Andrew Hamilton's Original Draught on Parchment

STATE HOUSE (INDEPENDENCE HALL), Philadelphia. 1732. The Hall

STATE HOUSE (INDEPENDENCE HALL), Philadelphia. 1732. Arch into Stair Tower

STATE HOUSE (INDEPENDENCE HALL), Philadelphia. 1732. Doorway to Independence Chamber

(*Top*) CHRIST CHURCH, Philadelphia. 1727. Spire added 1754

(*Bottom*) STENTON, Philadelphia. 1728. South Front

(*Top*) STENTON, Philadelphia. 1728. Doorway

(*Bottom*) FRAUNCES'S TAVERN, New York City. 1719. Town House of the De Lanceys. Became a Tavern 1763

(*Top*) OLD COLONY HOUSE, Newport, Rhode Island. 1739. South Front

(*Bottom*) PHILIPSE MANOR HOUSE, Yonkers, New York. *ante* 1680. South Front

HOLLIS HALL, Harvard Yard, Cambridge, Massachusetts. c. 1764

HARVARD HALL, Harvard Yard, Cambridge, Massachusetts. c. 1764

OLD STATE HOUSE, Boston. 1710-13

THE PASTURES, Albany, New York. 1762. East Front.
Vestibule added c. 1795

MACPHAEDRIS-WARNER HOUSE, Portsmouth, New Hampshire. c. 1720

(*Top*) MASSACHUSETTS HALL, Harvard Yard, Cambridge, Massachusetts. 1720

(*Bottom*) LUDLOW HOUSE, Claverack, New York. 1786. South Front

MOUNT AIRY, Richmond County, Virginia. c. 1756. Garden Front

(*Top*) MONTPELIER, Prince George's County, Maryland. c. 1750. Garden Front

(*Bottom*) MOUNT CLARE, Baltimore. 1750. South Front

(*Top*) MOUNT PLEASANT, Fairmount Park, Philadelphia. 1761. West Front

(*Bottom*) MOUNT CLARE, Baltimore. 1750. North Front. Porch added c. 1760

44

(*Top*) MOUNT PLEASANT, Fairmount Park, Philadelphia. 1761. East Front and Dependencies

(*Bottom*) CLIVEDEN, Germantown, Philadelphia. 1763. South-west Front

POWEL HOUSE, Philadelphia, 1756. Ball Room

(*Top*) TOWN HALL AND MARKET, Newport, Rhode Island. 1761

(*Bottom*) FANEUIL HALL, Boston. 1742. Enlarged by Charles Bulfinch 1805

47

OLD FIRST BAPTIST CHURCH, Providence, Rhode Island. 1775

48

ST. PHILIP'S CHURCH, Charleston, South Carolina. 1718. (Reconstruction)

(*Top*) WHITEHALL, Anne Arundel County, Maryland. 1763. South-west Front

(*Bottom*) The same, West Portico. Upper floor added later

(*Top*) HAMMOND-HARWOOD HOUSE, Annapolis, Maryland. 1774. West Front

(*Bottom*) WHITEHALL, Anne Arundel County, Maryland. 1763. North-east Front

(*Top*) HAMMOND-HARWOOD HOUSE, Annapolis, Maryland. 1774. Doorway

(*Bottom*) The same, Garden Front

52

(*Top*) JOSEPH BROWN HOUSE (NOW COUNTING HOUSE OF MESSRS. BROWN & IVES), Providence, Rhode Island. 1774

(*Bottom*) HOLDEN CHAPEL, Harvard Yard, Cambridge, Massachusetts. 1754

JEREMIAH LEE HOUSE, Marblehead, Massachusetts. 1763. South Front

(*Top*) DUMBARTON HOUSE, Georgetown, D.C. *ante* 1750; altered, moved and enlarged c.1810. South Front

(*Bottom*) The same, Parlour

(*Top*) DUMBARTON HOUSE, Georgetown, D.C. *ante* 1750; altered, moved and enlarged c.1810. North Front

(*Bottom*) THE WOODLANDS, Philadelphia. As enlarged 1788. North Front

56

(*Top*) PENNSYLVANIA HOSPITAL, Philadelphia. 1755-96. Central Building and West Wing (1796-1804);
West Wing corresponds with East Wing of 1755

(*Bottom*) HOMEWOOD, Baltimore. 1801. East Front

HOMEWOOD, Baltimore. 1801. Portico

HOUSE AT PORTSMOUTH, New Hampshire. c. 1798. Street Front

(*Top*) HARRISON GRAY OTIS HOUSE, Cambridge Street, Boston. c. 1795. South Front. *West Church* (Right)

(*Bottom*) PINGREE HOUSE, Salem, Massachusetts. c. 1800

60

(*Top*) BULFINCH STATE HOUSE, Boston. 1795

(*Bottom*) GORE PLACE, Waltham, Massachusetts. c. 1805. Garden Front

61

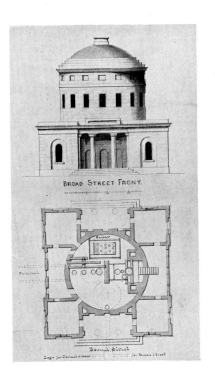

(*Top*) CENTRE SQUARE PUMPING STATION, Philadelphia. 1800. B.H. Latrobe's Elevation and Plan

(*Bottom*) The same, designed by Latrobe

62